LARRY SWAIM, TH.D.

WICKED OR WORTHY

21st Century Christian

Wicked or Worthy
ISBN: 978-0-89098-948-7

©2025 by 21st Century Christian, Inc
Nashville, TN 37215
All rights reserved.

All rights reserved. No part of this publication may be reproduced, stored in a retrieval system, or transmitted in any form or by any means—electronic, mechanical, photocopy, recording, digital, or otherwise—without the written permission of the publisher.

Unless otherwise noted, Scripture quotations are from the ESV® Bible (The Holy Bible, English Standard Version®), © 2001 by Crossway, a publishing ministry of Good News Publishers. Used by permission. All rights reserved.

Scripture quotations marked (NKJV) are taken from the New King James Version®. Copyright © 1982 by Thomas Nelson. Used by permission. All rights reserved.

Cover design by Jared Kendall

Acknowledgements

Thanks to Cathy Brown for her valuable help in proofreading and editing.

Dedication

This book is dedicated to Cathy Brown, who has worked with me on the manuscripts of seven books. They are *Faith: the Christian's Hope and Shield*, *The Christian and Good Mental Health*, *Growing Older in God's Grace*, *Set in Stone: A Study of God's Commandments*, and this title, *Wicked or Worthy*.

Cathy is a former assistant editor for 21st Century Christian, having worked on books by F. LaGard Smith, Denell Dennis, Harold Shank, the late Casandra Martin, the late Prentice Meador, and many others. Her proofreading, editing, and transcribing have been invaluable to me in writing these books. She has always surprised me by making the little (and sometimes big) corrections that make what I have written read better.

She is married to Eric Brown, a financial advisor, and has four sons: Doug, Daniel, Hunter, and Heath, and two daughters-in-law, Hannah Ruth and Emily. She has great talent, and I appreciate her using it in helping to get my books published.

Table of Contents

Explanation 9
Introduction 11
CHAPTER ONE ....
    Definitions, Explanation of Terms, and Chapter Synopses 13
CHAPTER TWO ....
    The Sin of Pride/Gluttony 21
CHAPTER THREE ....
    The Virtue of Humility 33
CHAPTER FOUR ....
    The Sin of Lust 45
CHAPTER FIVE ....
    The Virtue of Purity 55
CHAPTER SIX ....
    The Sin of Sloth 65
CHAPTER SEVEN ....
    The Virtue of Work 77
CHAPTER EIGHT ....
    The Sin of Greed 85
CHAPTER NINE ....
    The Virtue of Generosity 97
CHAPTER TEN ....
    The Sin of Envy 109
CHAPTER ELEVEN ....
    The Virtue of Peace 117
CHAPTER TWELVE ....
    The Sin of Anger/Wrath 129
CHAPTER THIRTEEN ....
    The Virtue of Patience 139

Bibliography 147

Explanation

The title of the book may cause concern for some in that we can never be worthy of God's grace, mercy, love, and salvation. This is true. Nothing we can ever do or say, no act of kindness, mercy, or grace on our part — no amount of work — can ever earn our salvation or make us worthy of the great sacrifice with which our Lord has blessed us.

However, there is another sense in which the word can be used that helps us understand that we can walk in a worthy manner: "You will do well to send them on their journey in a manner worthy of God" (3 John 6). "Walk in a manner worthy of God, who calls you into his own kingdom and glory" (1 Thessalonians 2:12). "Walk in a manner worthy of the Lord, fully pleasing to him: bearing fruit in every good work and increasing in the knowledge of God" (Colossians 1:10). "Only let your manner of life be worthy of the gospel of Christ" (Philippians 1:27). "I . . . urge you to walk in a manner worthy of the calling to which you have been called" (Ephesians 4:1).

These passages have nothing to do with merit on our part, but each points out the appreciation and faithfulness we should have for what God has done for us by doing what He asks of us. In no way do we deserve anything from the Lord. The passage from Colossians 1:10 answers the question about why we are to walk worthily, "Walk in a manner worthy of the Lord, *fully pleasing to him.*" Everything we do, believe, and say should be done for this very reason — to be pleasing to the Lord. Hebrews 11:6 teaches, "Without faith, it is impossible to please him [God]." Our faith is a demonstration of our desire to walk worthily in pleasing Him. Every attitude and action of the Christian should be directed toward walking worthily to please God.

Introduction

NEWTON'S THIRD LAW OF PHYSICS STATES, "FOR EVERY ACTION, there is an equal and opposite reaction." This is true not only in the physical world, but in the spiritual world as well. One cannot doubt the existence of both good and evil. In our daily lives, we see examples of both. We are inspired by sacrificial good, and we are harmed by indiscriminate evil. Throughout the Bible the drama plays out between good and evil, right and wrong, godliness and sin. It is easy to see the difference between the two, but much more difficult to choose good over evil, especially if we are deceived by the distorted lies of Satan, promising what he will not deliver and offering the opposite of his promises.

God's Word defines for us what is evil and what is good. It also outlines the consequences and results of both choices. We have but to look at the examples that are chronicled in both the Old and New Testaments to see the good and bad of people's choices and the ultimate results of choosing Satan's way over God's way. In this study, we will take what some have called the "Seven Deadly Sins," dissect them, and offer their equal and opposite reaction — the virtue that counters each deadly sin. In the fourth century, Jerome, most well-known as the father of the Latin Bible, catalogued what he considered to be the seven most deadly sins. We are all aware that all sin is deadly, but his view was that these were not only the deadliest of sins, but also the most common of sins. In Proverbs 6:16–19, God through inspiration lists seven sins He hates.

"There are six things that the Lord hates, seven that are an abomination to him: haughty eyes, a lying tongue, and hands that shed innocent blood, a heart that devises wicked plans, feet that make haste to run to evil, a false witness who breathes out lies, and one who sows discord among brothers." These sins are not the only sins mentioned in the Bible, but they do indicate those that are most offensive to God. These sins are at the root of a person's heart and motives when responding to the events of life.

The Ten Commandments are another listing of sins to be avoided and attitudes to be developed. In the Sermon on the Mount (Matthew 5:21–48), Jesus distinguishes between the actual sin and the condition of a person's heart. It is possible to sin without ever committing the sinful act. The instant we determine to commit sin if given the opportunity, it becomes sin. For this study, I have selected seven of the most common sins and seven of the most obvious virtues that are opposite to these sins. These are some of the dos and don'ts set forth by inspiration in God's holy Word. The sins and virtues chosen for this study are:

Pride/Gluttony and Humility
Lust and Purity
Sloth and Work
Greed and Generosity
Envy and Contentment
Anger/Wrath and Peace

CHAPTER ONE

Definitions, Terms, and Synopses of Each Chapter

Pride [prahyd]: "an inflated view of oneself without concern for others."

> "The fear of the LORD is hatred of evil. Pride and arrogance and the way of evil and perverted speech I hate" (Proverbs 8:13).
>
> "Pride goes before destruction, and a haughty spirit before a fall" (Proverbs 16:18).
>
> "For if anyone thinks he is something, when he is nothing, he deceives himself" (Galatians 6:3).

Pride, as it is played out in our lives, is seen in extreme self-centeredness, boastfulness, and an air of superiority. Pride often takes undeserved credit for the accomplishment of others or the inspiration and information given to us by others. Whatever successes we have may be partly because of good parents, teachers, friends and acquaintances, church members who invest time and effort to teach us God's Word, and peers who are willing to acknowledge and encourage our talents and abilities. But success, whatever it may mean to us individually, is never achieved entirely or exclusively by oneself. Of course, giving credit to God is one way of acknowledging that our pride is in check.

We should each have a reasonable self-image, one that is neither inflated nor deflated, but is completely in touch with our reality. We should seek out the talents and abilities God has invested in us and use them for the benefit of others, the glory of God, and our own contentment.

Humility [hyoo-mil-i-tee]: **a low or reasonable view of one's own importance.** Humility is freedom from pride and arrogance. Many excellent examples of humility are in the Bible: Daniel, Joseph, Ruth, Noah, Barnabas, the Good Samaritan, among others. Humility is a quality that is admired by most reasonable people and is a quality to be desired by anyone. See Colossians 3:12; 1 Peter 5:6, 7; Ephesians 4:2; and James 4:6, 10.

Greed [greed]: **an excessive and unprincipled pursuit of material wealth.** Hebrews 13:5 admonishes, "Keep your life free from love of money, and be content with what you have, for he has said, 'I will never leave you nor forsake you.'" Greed indicates a lack of faith in God's ability and willingness to help provide for us. Working and earning does not relieve us of the responsibility to provide for ourselves through the grace of God. Greed corrupts our motive for possessing material goods. This sin can be experienced by the rich as well as the poor. Many poor people are as greedy as those who have exploited people and circumstances to accumulate wealth. Greed is a form of hoarding — holding onto and storing things for the sake of simply possessing them. A greedy person sees other people as stepping stones and dispensable when they have served whatever purpose the greedy person requires.

Generosity **[jen-uh-ros-i-tee]*:* the quality of being kind.** *Liberality, magnanimity,* and *benevolence* are all synonyms for *generosity,* which means giving liberally of your financial assets, your time, and your talent. It a quality or fact of being a giving person, often to the point of sacrifice. Malachi 3:10–12 indicates that giving is the one thing God tells us to test Him in. We cannot out-give God. Giving is a test of our faith. God loved us so much that He gave His only Son to die for us. Generosity is proof positive of unselfishness. Generosity is a quality of helping others who may have less than you or be in greater need than you. It is a readiness to give to someone in need. A seldom-used synonym for generosity is *largesse* — the virtue of being unattached to material possessions and parting with them if needed to the benefit of others.

Sloth **[slawth]*:* continuous laziness, the failure to do what is needed for self-preservation and to assist others.** It is a waste of one's time and talents. Consider Proverbs 6:6: "Go to the ant, O sluggard; consider her ways, and be wise." Laziness is the opposite of wisdom. It is a foolish lifestyle. See the following passages: Proverbs 13:4; Proverbs 24:33, 34; Romans 12:11–13; Colossians 3:23; and 2 Thessalonians 3:10.

Only an understanding of God's plan that work makes us complete and gives us a legitimate feeling of self-worth will assist in overcoming sloth.

Work: **Activity involving mental, physical, or spiritual effort, done to achieve an intended result.** The only thing I would add to this definition would be "an intended *good purpose or* result." Synonyms are *labor, toil, effort,* or *slog.*

Man was designed to work so that he might have a feeling of purpose and destiny. There is a part of man that can only be satisfied by work. God expects us all to do good works to support ourselves and to help one another.

***Lust* [luhst]: a strong passion or longing, especially related to sexual desire.** Many believe that sexual desire is second only in intensity to the need and desire for food and water. Sexual desire is strong because it is God's way of encouraging procreation. As we saw with pride and gluttony, and as we will see with all the sins we discuss, there is a fine line between the good benefit of each action and the distortion and misuse that makes it become sin. Lust is spotlighted in Job 31:1; Matthew 5:28; Philippians 4:8; James 1:14, 15; 1 Peter 2:11; and John 2:16. The opposite of lust is purity, self-control, or chastity. We must control our passions and desires as God intends. Adultery is the contamination of God's pure intention for the sexual relationship and marriage.

***Purity* [pyoor-i-tee]: freedom from adulteration or contamination.** Synonyms are *cleanness*, *freshness*, *lack of pollution*, and *untainted*. From a spiritual point of view, it means freedom from immorality, especially sexual immorality. The opposite of purity is anything that debases us, contaminates us, pollutes us, or adds any kind of evil to our lives. Purity causes us to avoid inappropriateness, to be careful in our conversation and expression, clean in our heart, and virtuous in our thoughts. Being pure in heart is our constant struggle.

***Envy* [en-vee]: a relentless desire to have something someone else possesses and to wish the other person did not possess it.** "A tranquil life gives life to the flesh, but envy makes the bones rot" (Proverbs 14:30). Scriptures that speak of envy include James 3:14–16; Galatians 5:26; Proverbs 24:19, 20; Psalm 37:1; and Job 5:2.

Consideration and compassion for others are important qualities in overcoming envy. Being at peace with God and with all your acquaintances will be helpful in battling the sin of envy. If you can find peace and contentment in what you have instead of constantly wanting what someone else has (and wanting them not to have it), you will win the battle to overcome envy.

Unfortunately, we envy the most ridiculous things. Our neighbor gets a new car, and we wonder, *How do they do that? How can they afford it, and I can't?* We wish we had their car, and we wish they didn't have one. A friend gets a new swimming pool, tennis court, or builds an addition to their home, and envy begins to creep in. *I am as good as they are. Why can't I have these things?* And we begin to resent the other person for their good fortune, rather than rejoicing with those who rejoice and being happy for the good fortune of others. The sad part is that even if we had what we envy, it still would not bring us happiness, contentment, or peace.

***Peace* [pēs]*: **a state of tranquility; quietness or stillness.** This is one virtue we all need. It involves freedom from conflict, war, and agitation. It is a state of harmony, accord, goodwill, friendship, non-aggression, and non-violence. It is sorely needed in our world. We need peace with others and peace with God. Inner peace is a state of being mentally and spiritually at complete calmness. It involves the ability to be strong amid stress, discord, and faction. It is one of those qualities that is opposite to anxiety. We all seek a harmonious well-being and freedom from aggression. We all need to feel a freedom from violence. To find peace in the middle of life's storms and battles is truly a God thing.

***Wrath* [rath]*: **One of the most intense of all feelings, it involves hatred and contempt toward another person.** Romans 12:19 warns us: "Beloved, never aveng yourselves, but leave it to the wrath of God, for it is written, 'Vengeance is mine, I will repay, says the Lord.'"

God will avenge every wrongdoing committed by any unrepentant person. He alone is able to judge perfectly. We, as human beings, do not understand all circumstances involved in any act. God sees every facet, understands the motive of every heart, and will make fair judgments. Other passages to discuss include Proverbs 14:29, 15:1; Ephesians 4:26, 27; Colossians 3:8; and James 1:19, 20.

We avoid wrath and vengeance by understanding that God is the only being able to make a completely fair judgment and issue fair punishment for any deed of man. Unfortunately, most people want to take their vengeance immediately. Impatience has caused many people to act hastily and suffer grave consequences for their angry and wrathful actions. It is best that we leave consequential judgments to God and let Him decide the punishment.

Patience [pey-shuhns]: **the capacity to accept or tolerate delay or suffering without getting angry, upset, or seeking revenge.** It involves forbearance, tolerance, restraint, resignation, and endurance. It allows us to bear the annoyances, misfortunes, provocations, and delays without complaint, loss of temper, or irritation. Occasionally, we may find ourselves desperately in need of patience, and it's certainly a virtue because it is a state of moral excellence. It is one of those difficult qualities to achieve and maintain. So many conflicts could be avoided if we were more patient.

For examples of scriptural emphasis of patience, see Romans 8:24–30; Ephesians 4:2; Psalm 37:7–9; Ephesians 4:2; Proverbs 15:18; and Romans 12:12. Once you have mastered the virtue of patience, you are at the epitome of spiritual maturity.

Gluttony [gluht-n-ee]: **a sin of excess, of opulence, of the desire to have only the best regardless of the cost.** It is inseparably attached to pride. Many people resort to stealing or buying things they cannot afford and ultimately must relinquish. Even if one becomes successful in the world and is able to maintain the opulent lifestyle — the gadgets and gimmicks, the glitter and gleam ("eye candy") — they will never give us what we are actually seeking, for this supposedly superior lifestyle is only a lie from Satan.

Contentment [kuhn-tent-muhnt]: **a state of happiness or satisfaction.** Spiritually, contentment comes from following Christ and having faith in Him that we will have everything we need, that Christ is sufficient, and that His promises are true and always enough. Explore examples in Philippians 4:11–13; 1 Timothy 6:6–12; 2 Corinthians 12:9, 10; Romans 8:28; and Proverbs 19:23. There are people who have no peace of mind, who would pay thousands of dollars if they could find contentment. If only they knew that contentment is free and from the Lord.

This brief introduction to each of the deadly sins and life-giving virtues we will study is meant to give us an idea of what we can expect from this study. My prayer is that it will be a blessing to you.

CHAPTER TWO

The Sins of Pride and Gluttony

DEADLY SINS. AREN'T ALL SINS DEADLY? YES. THERE IS NO SIN that does not result in spiritual death unless it (and the sinner) is forgiven, and all of us are going to die physically because we sin. Some sins, however, are so broad and have such deep roots that they affect other sins.

As I have gotten older, I try to make my writing as urgent, contemporary, and useful as possible. We live in a difficult time. Our world has changed; it has become confused and divided. Sometimes it seems as if we are rushing headlong toward a cliff, an abyss, from which there is no return.

Having said that, though, what could be more urgent or more needed than for us to understand God's Word and for us to have an outline of sins to be avoided and virtues to be imitated. To that end, we will vascillate between deadly sins and their antitheses. For example, in this lesson, we will study pride, and in the next chapter, we'll look at humility.

Pride is one of the deadliest sins of our day. We try to make things easier to understand. We try to bring clarity to difficult or complex situations. We want to know the best and the worst. On one occasion, someone went to Jesus after He had given an illustration about being a good neighbor and asked, "Who is my neighbor?" (Luke 10:29). The man might as well have asked Jesus to define it for him. We try to justify our mistakes, failure, and sins in one way or another.

The disciples were together on one occasion and began to ask, "Who is the greatest among us?" wanting to know their rank among Jesus' followers. Then there was the person who went to Jesus asking, "Which is the greatest commandment of all?" At the time he asked that question, there were more than 600 laws in Israel. Which one was the greatest? I sometimes think we ask this to justify our being unwilling to follow God's will.

Sins are deadly. There are some branches of Christianity who divide sin into two categories: mortal (or deadly) sins and venal (or corrupt) sins. One is deadly, and the other isn't necessarily deadly, but it's still bad. The Bible, however, makes no such division. Scripture is clear that all sin brings about death. We are to avoid sin. Sin is missing the mark. Sin separates us from one another and from God.

These are the sins we'll study in this book: pride, gluttony, envy, greed, lust, sloth (laziness), and anger. Certainly, looking at this list we understand they are deadly sins. They are not mentioned in the Bible all together, but they are individually highlighted throughout the Word.

Sin first raised its ugly head in the Garden of Eden. Pride was the culprit behind the first sin Pride is a broad sin. It encompasses not only this sin, but reaches out and presses people to commit all kinds of other sins, too. People lie, steal, cheat, commit adultery, and murder because of pride. Once we give our hearts over to pride, the door is open to many other sins.

The Bible says that God hates pride. Read these examples.

> "Everyone proud in heart is an abomination to the Lord; Though they join forces, none will go unpunished" (Proverbs 16:5, NKJV).
>
> "A man's pride will bring him low, But the humble in spirit will retain honor" (Proverbs 29:23, NKJV).
>
> "God resists the proud, but gives grace to the humble" (James 4:6, NKJV).

It is important to understand that pride is a sin that causes many problems and difficulties, separates us from one another, and certainly separates us from God. It is much more serious than we often think.

It has been a long time since I have heard a lesson on pride or on any of the sins classified as the "seven deadly sins." We must realize that pride is a sin. Pride is defined in a good way as "a feeling of self-respect, a feeling of self-worth." We should all have a healthy respect for God's giving us life. There is, though, an unreasonable, innate self-esteem. There are synonyms to accompany it, too: conceit, egotism, self-importance, self-love, vanity, narcissism. All these describe this condition that, when we see it in others, we resist and dislike it, but we are so often unable to see it in ourselves.

C.S. Lewis said, "Pride is the great sin." Then he went on to say, "According to the great Christian theologians and teachers of the past, the utmost evil, one of the worst of all the sins, is pride. Unchastity (or lust), anger, greed, drunkenness, all of these, he says, are mere little 'fleabites' when one compare them to pride. The other sins are individual, but pride affects everything we think about, talk about, act upon, or live."

Lewis went on to say, "The devil became the devil because of pride, when he was cast out of heaven. Pride leads to every other vice and sin. The complete anti-God state of mind is uncontrolled pride."

Pride is one of those sins that we must avoid at all costs. It is amazing where we sometimes find good information and advice. Roger Miller wrote these lyrics in 1966, "It's my belief pride is the chief cause in the decline in the number of husbands and wives." And that is true. Once pride enters, it affects even our closest relationships.

The reason C.S. Lewis wrote that pride is among the worst of sins is because since the beginning, even going back into the Old Testament, many biblical scholars attested that this is an intrusive, disruptive, and deadly sin. Josephus, the great historian, spoke of pride as being one of the great sins. Augustine and others taught that the sin of pride will easily entrap us. Calvin, Luther, Wesley, Knox, Thomas Campbell — all put pride at the top of the list of all of our sins.

Pride caused Lucifer the Light Bearer, the one who thought of himself as equal to God, who tried to rival God, to be cast out of heaven. The event is told in Isaiah 14:12–15 (NKJV): "How you are fallen from heaven, O Lucifer, son of the morning! How you are cut down to the ground, You who weakened the nations! For you have said in your heart: 'I will ascend to heaven, I will exalt my throne above the stars of God; I will also sit on the mount of the congregation on the farthest sides of the north; I will ascend above the heights of the clouds, I will be like the Most High.' Yet you shall be brought down to Sheol, to the lowest depths of the Pit." He says five times, "I will," which is, of course, an indication of his pride.

That is a description of Lucifer, who thought he was able to become God, but could not. As a result of being cast down to the earth, he began his insidious attack on every one of God's creatures. He wants to lead us away from God, our Creator. He is working today among all of us to discourage us, defeat us, and cause us to become less like God.

In Genesis 3:1–5 (ESV), we find out how pride was involved in the first sin and extends to this very day. "Now the serpent was more crafty than any other beast of the field that the Lord God had made. He said to the woman, 'Did God actually say, "You shall not eat of any tree in the garden?"' and the woman said to the serpent, 'We may eat of the fruit of the trees in the garden, but God said, "You shall not eat of the fruit of the tree that is in the midst of the garden, neither shall you touch it, lest you die."' But the serpent said to the woman, 'You will *not* surely die. For God knows that when you eat of it your eyes will be opened, and you will be like God, knowing good and evil.'"

He changes only one word. *Do you see how beautiful that fruit is? Do you want it? Can you see how good it will taste? It will satisfy your body, and it will make you as wise as God.* And so the deception begins, and here Eve is introduced for the first time to being able to doubt God. God created her and put her in a perfect circumstance, but even that was not good enough when tempted by pride. As a result, Eve began to question whether God really had her best interests at heart. The devil says to us, "God wants to keep you from having fun." So Eve took the fruit, ate it, and gave some to her husband, Adam. Their eyes were opened, and they became aware of sin for the first time. Notice the subtlety of what takes place here.

It sounds like an exaggeration to say that pride can lead to almost every other sin — but it does. There are some who are proud of their looks, and consequently, they feel they can have anyone and anything they want at any time. Other have pride in their intellect, in their abilities and talents, in their athletic prowess, or in their careers. when that pride takes over, and you do things to be seen of men and not for God, that is sin. We need to be willing to do what we do, using the gifts we have, to the glory and honor of God.

I have said this on several occasions, especially when I was younger, "The worst thing you can do for me, or anyone, is to give too many compliments." Once we start believing that we may be gifted in some way or another, that may lead us away from the Lord. First Corinthians 4:5–7 exhorts, "Therefore do not pronounce judgment before the time, before the Lord comes, who will bring to light the things now hidden in darkness and will disclose the purposes of the heart. Then each one will receive his commendation from God. I have applied all these things to myself and Apollos for your benefit, brothers, that you may learn by us not to go beyond what is written, that none of you may be puffed up in favor of one against another. For who sees anything different in you? What do you have that you did not receive? If then you received it, why do you boast as if you did not receive it?"

Do you have athletic ability? Can you sing beautifully? Do you have other talents and abilities? Where did those come from? You may have honed them, you may have exemplified them, but God gave them to you. What do you have that you did not receive? You probably had little to do with the talents, abilities, and appearance God gifted you. He gives people talents and abilities to use in His kingdom and to help others.

"That you may learn by us not to go beyond what is written, that none of you may be puffed up...." (1 Corinthians 4:6). Don't become proud because of what you have received, but graciously acknowledge God as the giver of everything good you have. "Each person is tempted when he is lured and enticed by his own desire. Then desire when it has conceived gives birth to sin, and sin when it is fully grown brings forth death" (James 1:14–15).

Gluttony

Gluttony is one of the great sins of our day, but it isn't just related to food. It is a way of life, of wanting the best of everything. We have a word for this gluttonous appetite and spirit: materialism; that is, wanting the finest and the best that we can possibly have. Again, pride is involved!

Back to Eve. Notice how arrogant Satan is when he tempts her. He arrogantly contradicts God, and he says to Eve "If you eat this fruit, you will *not* die. Rather, if you eat, you will become like God." How many of us would like to become like God — to be able to choose what we do, when we do it, or how we do it? How many of us would like to be able to do things with no consequences? But God, who created us, understands us even better than we understand ourselves. The God who made everything has given us exactly what is best for us. The further we drift from God's plan, the closer we get to the consequences of our neglect. When we begin to let pride take over, there is an *inversion* of our attitudes toward God. As we let pride eat away at our soul, God becomes smaller, and we become bigger. As God becomes smaller, we listen to Him less. We are unwilling to follow Him as we once did. It is now a matter of every man doing what is right in his own eyes (Judges 21:25). *I'll do what I want to do. God doesn't understand what I am going through.* But God does understand everything. We can't always understand or comprehend God's plan, but God does!

One of the great facts of life is that power, which comes with pride, corrupts. Absolute power corrupts absolutely. To a person who is a king or dictator, their word is law. They can do and have anything they want. This incredible power feeds their ego and pride, and they begin to think of themselves as a god. Many kings of the past declared themselves to be divine. This occurred even as late as World War II, when the emperor of Japan declared himself to be a deity. We know, though, that try as we may, we can never become like God. "All have sinned and fall short of the glory of God" (Romans 3:23). "None is righteous, no, not one" (Romans 3:10). There isn't anyone who can say that they have never sinned or done anything contrary to the will of God. We understand our humanity, our faults, and our failures. That alone should be enough to humble us and help us to realize that we have no reason to be inordinately proud, and we have every reason to be humble. The best among us have flaws and faults, warts and wrinkles. Every one of us has failed in many ways.

Eve began to doubt God, and when we begin to doubt that God means what He says, that His Word is absolute and without fault, that God loves us, cares about us, and understands what we are going through — when we doubt all this, that is when we are in Satan's clutches because of pride. Ensnared by pride and self-deception, Eve gives in. In a few perfect moves by Satan, she has gone from believing, trusting, and living in Paradise, to disbelieving, distrusting, disobeying God, and being cast out of the Garden.

Before we are too hard on Eve, let's look at our own lives. We fall prey to the same subtle temptations that tangled Eve. Jesus was even tempted in the wilderness in these same ways, yet He did not sin. Conversely, we are tempted in the same ways, but we *do* sin. From this point on in the Bible, we can see Satan having his way in the lives of individuals, nations, and cultures. We worship and study to find better ways to avoid the angry darts of Satan, to find out how to put on the armor of God so that we can repel Satan's efforts. As Christians, we draw closer to one another, depending on each other to point out when we might be tempted to leave God.

> When pride is involved, people often give up on God.

I hope that God is as important in your life as He ever was, and pray that your faith is as strong as it ever has been. But I do know that pride creeps in and entangles us. Pride-filled people can become gluttonous. The more they have, whether it is material blessings, power, or authority, the more they want. Finally, when pride is involved, people often give up on God — individually, culturally, and nationally. They begin to become their own gods, doing things their own way. That power of pride causes them to abuse or neglect others. We see it every day in politics, business, and even in our own lives. When we get a little of anything, it never seems to be enough. We want more and better, even when what we have should make us content. We keep striving, thinking we will find something to fill that hole in our soul, when the only thing that will ever fill it is God, our Creator.

There are many biblical examples of this happening. Consider Uzziah who rose to the throne in Judah at age 16. "As long as he sought the Lord, God made him prosper" (2 Chronicles 26:5). When he first came to power, he depended on Zechariah the prophet for mentoring and advice. Zechariah led him in the ways of God. Then we read a sad commentary on the corruption of pride and power, which came later. "And his fame spread far, for he was marvelously helped, till he was strong. But when he was strong, he grew proud, to his destruction" (2 Chronicles 26:15, 16). This is what happens. We begin to think more of ourselves than we should. We think we are stronger than we really are, or better, or more talented, which causes us to stumble and fall.

Sometimes we are chastised by God because we have fallen. But this may be the best thing to happen to us. When we lose something we value, that may be God's way of saying, "You can't do it by yourself. You're going to mess it up if you try." We should humbly go to God in prayer and say, "Thank you for everything you've given me, and I want to use all that you have given me for your glory and honor. I seek no glory for myself. I give you the glory and honor because you have given me everything that is good." We should pass on the credit to God. It was never ours. We should never try to claim it for ourselves, expecting others to think highly of us for what we have done.

Having been a therapist for 30+ years, I have seen pride involved in many psychological problems. In fact, many of the worst psychological problems have their root connection to pride.

Narcissism is inseparably bound to a proud spirit. For the narcissist and the neurotic, everything revolves around them. No matter what happens in their lives, their first question is, "How will it affect me?" Even sometimes when they admit they may be wrong, it is because they want someone to disagree and say they aren't wrong.

I am quoting from the head of the psychology department at Harvard University, "The neurotic disorder is tied directly to pride. . . . From the point of view of religion and of psychology, pride is the root of most, if not all, neuroses." C.S. Lewis said, "Pride is a cancer that eats up the very possibility of our loving each other, loving God, and loving ourselves as we ought to. It even eats up common sense." If your pride causes you to exalt yourself, you need to be careful. If you become so proud that you think you have arrived, you have just painted a target on your back for God. God says that He will bring low the proud. In the next chapter, we'll see why humility is better than pride. Pride says, "I can get along without God." Pride causes us to do the right thing for the wrong reasons. Pride says, "I believe the lies of Satan more than I believe the truth of God." Pride says, "I know much more than God, so I choose to lust, to lie, to steal, to cheat, to be proud." It is all an attempt for each of us individually to become our own god. Over the years, I have talked to people who say, "I know that's what God's Word says, but I think God wants me to be happy." Their actions might bring them a little pleasure, but if it's wrong, if it's a sin, it will work out badly in the long run.

We set ourselves above God. We make choices in which we are actually saying, "I know more than God. God doesn't understand. God doesn't know me." We finally get to the point that we doubt God loves us, even though in hundreds of places in the Bible, God shows over and over that He loves us and wants what's best for us.

It is important to take self-inventory, to look inside our hearts and our minds, and see where we are. If we repent of our sins, acknowledging them and asking God to forgive us, He will forgive us through the blood of His Son, Jesus. He will help us to do His will.

God showed His love for us in sending Jesus to us. He gave His only Son to die for us. Think about that! Every sin we have ever committed, every wrong thought, and every immoral action can be erased. God will never hold it against us. Instead, we often struggle under the load of our pride, guilt, and sin, until the day we die. We fail to recognize that it may be a heavy load here, but it is a much heavier load hereafter. I hope and pray that as we go through this study, you will realize that God loves you, He knows what is best, and He wants you to come to Him on His terms, not yours.

> "It was pride that changed angels into devils; it is humility that makes men as angels." —AUGUSTINE

QUESTIONS

1. Explain how all sins are deadly.

2. Discuss how some sins have more earthly consequences than others.

3. Discuss how pride is such a deadly sin.

4. How does pride sometimes lead to other sins?

5. What led to the first sin?

6. Discuss why the devil's great sin was pride.

7. How does Satan use pride to lead us away from God?'

8. How can the ability and talents God has given us sometimes become a stumbling block?

9. Why is gluttony often evidence of too much pride?

10. Why is choosing an excessive, opulent lifestyle often motivated by pride?

11. What are some biblical examples of pride?

12. How is pride sometimes involved in mental or emotional problems?

CHAPTER THREE

The Virtue of Humility

PRIDE IS THE ROOT OF MANY OTHER SINS. PRIDE SEPARATES us from God, probably more often than any other sin. Why? It's because pride diminishes God and elevates self. Pride causes us to want to do things our way, believing the lies of Satan when he says, "You won't die, you won't be hurt, sin won't bother you, God is trying to keep you from pleasure." We buy into these excuses, and that's unfortunate.

In this chapter we will study the opposite of pride: humility. Humility involves being willing to acknowledge that God is God, and that we are His creation, not the Creator. God knows what is best, and if we follow His words and His will, our lives will be better than any other life choice.

Humility and wisdom can come from unexpected sources, including this anonymous quote that makes a lot of sense: "If you can start the day without caffeine, if you can always be cheerful, ignoring all the aches and pains that you may have, if you can resist complaining and boring people with your troubles, if you can eat the same food every day and be thankful and grateful for it, if you can understand when your loved ones are too busy to give you any time or attention, if you can take criticism without blame or resentment, if you can resist treating rich friends better than poor friends, if you can face the world without lies or deceit, if you can overlook it when loved ones take out their frustrations on you though it is no fault of yours, if you can conquer tension without medical help and pills, if you can say honestly deep within your heart you have no prejudice at all against any person then, my friends, you have become just as good as your dog." My wife and I recently got a new puppy. I have been getting up every morning at 4:30 since her arrival. One morning I looked down after I got to church and noticed both my shoestrings had been untied. Our pup is the cutest little she-devil ever, but she's already taught us so much about humility and patience, and if we are observant, we can see humility exemplified in many ways.

I don't know how you feel about yourself, but while researching this lesson, I came across a sermon described as, "Bar none, the very best sermon on humility ever preached by anyone." I hope that was tongue-in-cheek by that preacher! Humility is one of those qualities that we cannot claim for ourselves. I can say that I am loving, kind, compassionate, truthful, honest, and fair, but when I say to someone, "I am very, very humble," that doesn't go over well. You must have that quality recognized in you by other people rather than claiming it for yourself. In fact, if you claim to be humble, that's proof positive that you aren't.

Humility is a quality that we love to see in people. We watch how others live and the way they behave and what they do, and it makes us feel good when we see someone who is not too carried away with themselves. A well-known author wrote, "Humility is not thinking less of yourself; it is thinking of yourself less."

Humility is a virtue that we all need. At one time or another in our lives, we all get to the point that we think more highly of ourselves than we should. If something goes well in an area of our lives, we begin to think we are special, maybe more special than others. Then something comes along that reminds us we may be special in one area, but we are lacking in many others.

Humility is necessary. In fact, it is mentioned slightly fewer times than love in the Bible. God admires humility. God lifts the humble but brings the proud low (Matthew 23:12). Humility is a God-loved quality that we must develop in our own lives. We need to remember who we are and Whose we are. God made us and understands us. He knows our needs, wants, and desires. Most of all, He has provided for us an answer to those needs in His Word.

> God wants to use every one of us, all our talents and abilities and resources, but He also wants us to give Him the glory and honor, not taking it for ourselves.

God can't use us for great things as long we think we are better than anyone else. When we begin to think more highly of ourselves than we ought, then we begin to diminish God's ability to use us. God wants to use every one of us, all our talents and abilities and resources, but He also wants us to give Him the glory and honor, not taking it for ourselves. When we begin to take it for ourselves, we do not give God what is rightfully His. In the previous chapter, we reviewed Paul's words from 1 Corinthians 4:7, "For who sees anything different in you? What do you have that you did not receive? If then you received it, why do you boast as if you did not receive it?" When we use the gifts given to us by God for His glory, we become a blessing to Him. That is what we are supposed to be. We are not to have an inferiority complex, believing that we are worse than everyone else or that we have no value. We need to have a healthy respect for ourselves, mentally and spiritually, but we don't need to think we are better than anyone else. No matter how big your house is, somebody lives in a bigger one. Whatever kind of car you drive, someone drives a better one. However much money you make, somebody makes more. Comparing ourselves with others gets us in trouble. When we compare ourselves with others, then pride, jealousy, envy, and other sins begin to sweep in like a tidal wave because of our lack of humility. For me, humility is saying to God that everything I am and have and ever will be is His. He gave it to me, invested it in me, and allowed me to use it. I give Him the glory, honor, and credit for every good thing that may ever be accomplished.

When we are humble, God lifts us up and helps us. The main thing God gives us because of humility is *grace*. Does anyone not need God's grace? How many times a day do we fail and fall? How many times do we sin, hurting ourselves or someone else? Grace is one of the most neededqualities we can receive from God. The Bible says, "God opposes the proud but gives *grace* to the *humble*" (James 4:6, emphasis added). God resists the proud. I don't want to be resisted by God, do you? I want God to feel comfortable with what I am doing. We want God to be pleased that we are using what He has given us to His glory.

God welcomes the humble to be with Him in heaven. There are certain advantages to being humble that you cannot receive any other way. One is, "I dwell in the high and holy place, and also with him who is of a contrite and lowly spirit" (Isaiah 57:15). We get to dwell with God when we are humble.

I love to see somebody doing something well. I love to hunt and fish. When I am hunting with a good hunter who knows how to hunt, I brag on them. If there is an athlete who wins a race after much preparation and sacrifice, we give them credit for what they have accomplished and tell others. I also know people who have probably never given a compliment to anyone in their life, but they have given lots of criticism. There are times when we all need to be criticized, but there are also times we need to be complimented for doing what we should do as well as possible. God resists the proud, but gives grace to the humble.

God hears the prayers of the humble. "He does not forget the cry of the humble" (Psalm 9:12, NKJV). To go to God in prayer with a haughty, pride-filled, arrogant attitude probably means our prayers will not rise much higher than the ceiling. However, when we humble ourselves, and when we look at both sides of our accomplishments, considering how lacking we are in some areas, it ought to balance out and help us to realize that we have both advantages and disadvantages. If you lack humility, pray for it. God will provide. Remember, Paul had a "thorn in the flesh" to keep him humble.

As we walk through life, encountering pitfalls, obstacles, and all kinds of temptations, we need to know that God is there to guide us every step of the way. Pride will keep us from seeing who we really are and what our needs are.

Humility is a genuine lifestyle. It is not something we have one day and not the next. If we are truly humble, it will always be a part of us. We will constantly recognize who we are and where everything we have came from, giving thanks to God for it: "Walk in a manner worthy of the calling to which you have been called" (Ephesians 4:1). All of us are "walking," both figuratively and lliterally, every day. We are to walk in a manner worthy of our Christian faith, and in doing so we receive God's blessings. "Walking" refers to living our daily lives at church, on the job, at the store — wherever we are. We all like people who, wherever we see them, are always the same. That sameness comes from understanding who we are and what God wants us to be.

In humility and grace, God molds us into the people He can most effectively use. No matter who we are with, where we are, or what we are doing, we should exemplify humility. When we are at home with our family, we need to be humble. When we are on the job with our peers, we need to be humble. When we are enjoying ourselves at a social event, we need to be humble. We need to understand to the depth of our souls that we are God's created.

In the previous chapter, we learned that Satan became proud, challenged God, and was thrown out of heaven. That pride continues to infiltrate every one of us, to cause us to be proud, to diminish God in our sight. But we, knowing God and serving Him, want to be the best people and servants possible.

That certainly runs contrary to our current culture, which urges, "Succeed at any cost. It doesn't matter what it takes, just get there. Be who you want to be, do what you want to do, and live as you want to live. Be all you can be. Take charge, be aggressive, don't back down. Do whatever you have to do to succeed." That is the predominant message today, and it is a message couched in pride. We can achieve the epitome of our abilities and still be humble. We can do what we should do, and should want to do, and still be humble.

God says, "Do nothing from selfish ambition or conceit, but in humility count others more significant than yourselves" (Philippians 2:3). If you want to make your workplace environment better, start respecting your colleagues. Start helping and encouraging those who may be slackers. Start setting a good example for everyone by doing your job well while also doing it humbly. You will find that the atmosphere will immediately change.

"Clothe yourselves, all of you, with humility toward one another" (1 Peter 5:5). That simply means that, in the same way we put on clothes when we get ready to go out, we put on humility — we wear it, and it becomes a part of us. Also, it is something we can control. We can control whether we are proud and arrogant or whether we are humble and a blessing to others. I think we need to simply come to an understanding that we are not perfect and never will be. We must realize it is by the grace of God that we have anything at all, including forgiveness of all our sins. That should make us all humble. We never pull ourselves up by our own bootstraps and completely succeed if in doing so we become arrogant and proud. Rather, we should give credit to others for what they have done to help us get where we are — our parents, our siblings, our friends, teachers, and mentors. They are the ones who have spent time and energy to put a little piece of clay on us and help mold us into the kind of people we need to be. We take a lot from others, but how much do we give back? That's how we acknowledge what should be recognized in others, giving them credit.

Do you know who else can help mold us into the person each of us should be? The only example of perfection personified: Christ Himself.

Jesus is the perfect example of humility. No one was humbler than He. Jesus stepped down from His princely throne and threw off the robes of power. He was born in a stable, as lowly a place to be born as any. But He came not to be served; He came to serve. His whole life from beginning to end was about service. Wherever He went, He served. He fed, clothed, healed, and forgave people. He pointed us to God, the Father. In every situation, no matter how bleak, He said, "Father, thy will, not mine, be done." We should adopt that same attitude. We may want things to be a certain way, but we should remember, "Not my will, but Your will be done, Father." When we break our will to God's will, becoming humbly obedient, we are where Jesus was when He walked upon the earth.

Jesus grew up in a middle-class home, but even when He was young, He showed an attitude of humility and love toward God. When Jesus, as a young boy, left is parents and stayed in the temple listening to the teachers, He told His parents, "Did you not know that I must be about my Father's business?" (Luke 2:49, NKJV). The will of our Father in heaven is more important than any other relationship we may have. There will never be any relationship that is more important than our relationship with God. Having that good relationship makes all our other relationships better.

"He also told this parable to some who trusted in themselves that they were righteous and treated others with contempt: 'Two men went up into the temple to pray, one a Pharisee and the other a tax collector. The Pharisee, standing by himself, prayed thus: "God, I thank you that I am not like other men, extortioners, unjust, adulterers, or even like this tax collector. I fast twice a week; I give tithes of all that I get." But the tax collector, standing far off, would not even lift his eyes to heaven, but beat his breast, saying, "God, be merciful to me, a sinner!" I tell you, this man went down to his house justified, rather than the other. For everyone who exalts himself will be humbled, but the one who humbles himself will be exalted'" (Luke 18:9–14).

That is how Jesus said we are to live. On another occasion, He said, "When you are invited by someone to a wedding feast, do not sit down in a place of honor, lest someone more distinguished than you be invited by him, and he who invited you both will come and say to you, 'Give your place to this person,' and then you will begin with shame to take the lowest place. But when you are invited, go and sit in the lowest place, so that when your host comes he may say to you, 'Friend, move up higher.' Then you will be honored in the presence of all who sit at table with you" (Luke 14:7–10). The scary part about this passage to me is this: Jesus was criticizing the very people who should have been the best, the most righteous and godly, the most humble, yet they were the opposite. Yes, they were religious, but God was not proud of them. We need to be careful not to become a people of "religious-ocity," that we don't brag about who we are and what we do, but that we let our lives demonstrate our service and humility.

If your past sins don't keep you humble, nothing likely will. If your past failures don't remind you again and again that you are not as good as you think you are, then you are not paying attention to the past. To apply Jesus' teaching to our present-day culture, we don't need to be concerned about having the biggest and best of everything, about receiving the most praise. Instead, we should look to the words from Proverbs 27:2: "Let another praise you, and not your own mouth; a stranger, and not your own lips." When you start bragging on yourself and your accomplishments, that's when you may be close to getting in trouble. Jesus humbled Himself, even to death on the cross. Reread that passage of Scripture (John 13) about that final night: Jesus and His disciples had gathered in the upper room one last time. Jesus stood, took off His robe, and wrapped a towel around Himself. He then proceeded to wash the feet of each of the apostles, an act of incredible humility.

Instead of the disciples understanding what they should have known after three years of learning from Jesus, they were more concerned with what they would do after Jesus left. Peter even said, "You shall never wash my feet" (John 13:8). Jesus understood that Peter's mouth got away from him sometimes, but He still loved him. "Jesus answered him, 'If I do not wash you, you have no share with me.' Simon Peter said to him, 'Lord, not my feet only but also my hands and my head!' Jesus said to him, 'The one who has bathed does not need to wash, except for his feet, but is completely clean'" (John 13:8b–10). And Jesus knelt and washed Peter's feet. What an incredible act of humility!

Immediately after washing their feet, Jesus tells His apostles, "I have given you an example, that you also should do just as I have done to you. Truly, truly, I say to you, a servant is not greater than his master, nor is a messenger greater than the one who sent him. If you know these things, blessed are you if you do them. I am not speaking of all of you; I know whom I have chosen. But the Scripture will be fulfilled, 'He who ate my bread has lifted his heel against me'" (John 13:15–18). Here Jesus foreshadows His imminent betrayal by Judas. On another occasion, Jesus was at a feast and a harlot approached Him and fell before Him weeping, asking for His mercy.

She washed His feet with her own tears and with expensive ointment that she had brought, drying them with her hair (Luke 7:36–50).

Humility is not an easy trait to develop. It takes constant, daily reminding ourselves of who we are, what we should do, and how we need to live. "Have this mind among yourselves, which is yours in Christ Jesus, who, though he was in the form of God, did not count equality with God a thing to be grasped, but emptied himself, by taking the form of a servant, being born in the likeness of men. And being found in human form, he *humbled* himself by becoming obedient to the point of death, even death on a cross" (Philippians 2:5–8, emphasis added). If anyone ever had the right to think more highly of Himself than others, it was Jesus. But, as in every other example from His life, He taught us how to live. He showed humility. In Philippians, Paul is trying to encourage ordinary believers in the church. He wants them to have the same mind, the same humility, as Jesus. He writes the words to a regular body of believers, just like we are. He is telling us what our attitude should be, how we should think, and how we should feel about ourselves. He also emphasizes who gets the credit for what we do when it is done well and in keeping with God's will. Paul said it so that we wouldn't allow sinful pride to come in and take over, defeating us in our quest to become more like God through Jesus, reflecting and adopting the attitude that Jesus demonstrated all of His life.

"Therefore God has highly exalted him and bestowed on him the name that is above every name, so that at the name of Jesus every knee should bow, in heaven and on earth and under the earth, and every tongue confess that Jesus Christ is Lord, to the glory of God the Father" (Philippians 2:9–11). That comes right after the Scriptures tell us to put on the mind of Christ. As a psychotherapist, I have studied the mind most of my life. The more I study, the more I realize how little we know about the mind, but I do know we can change our mind. We can change our attitudes and the sinful conditions of our lives. We can become more Christ-like, and that begins with the acknowledgement of our sins. To solve the problem, we must first understand and admit the problem. Then there comes that moment of decision when we change our will. This is "conversion," and it is an extremely powerful moment in a person's life. You decide to walk in a different direction than you have before. Until you've had that experience and made up your mind to be, think, and act differently, change probably will never happen.

We should want to adopt the virtues and attributes that Jesus had. There is another component to this that we often overlook: the power of the Holy Spirit. I don't know all that the Holy Spirit can do or how it may affect people. But I say to God, "Father, I don't know all the Holy Spirit is to do in my life, but whatever it is supposed to do, I want it. I want the Holy Spirit living in me so that I can become the person I should be and live the kind of life I should live.

We have God, Jesus, and the Holy Spirit, and we have the Word. We know what we are supposed to do and how we are supposed to live. We know the virtues and qualities that we are to have. I pray we will be able to make the changes we need to make.

> "For who sees anything different in you? What do you have that you did not receive? If then you received it, why do you boast as if you did not receive it?" (1 Corinthians 4:7). Whatever talents and abilities you have are a gift from God. As we pray to Him, we thank Him for using the talents and abilities He gave us, and for His love, mercy, and grace.

QUESTIONS

1. Why is it difficult, if not impossible, to claim the quality of humility for ourselves?

2. Why does God punish the proud and elevate the humble?

3. Who is ultimately responsible for every talent or ability we possess?

4. What does our humility say about our understanding of our relationship to God?

5. Why is it a bad idea to compare ourselves to others?

6. How is humility an indication that we appreciate the talents, abilities, and successes of others?

7. How does pride keep us from seeing our real strengths and weaknesses?

8. Discuss Philippians 2:2, 3.

9. Discuss the pride and humility pictured in Luke 18:9–14.

10. How can an honest inventory of our own lives, with all the mistakes and sins we have committed, help keep us humble?

11. Discuss Jesus' example of washing the apostles' feet as an example of humility.

12. Why should we be humble in view of 1 Corinthians 4:7?

CHAPTER FOUR

The Sin of Lust

LUST IS CERTAINLY A DEADLY SIN, DESTROYING MANY HOMES and lives. For that reason, we want to learn all we can about how to avoid this temptation. When we hear the word *lust* we usually think of sexual sins. But if you go back in both the Hebrew and the Greek, the word has a much broader meaning. In fact, the Greek has six different words that are used for the one word *lust*. Paul wrote to the Thessalonians about his "great desire" to see them (1 Thessalonians 2:17), and the same word translated here as "desire" is translated elsewhere as "lust." There are other passages where this occurs, and we can learn from this that it is the context of the sentence that determines which English word is used. The words *covet, desire, want,* and *lust* are all translated from the same Greek word: *epithumia*.

Christ desires that each one of us know, understand, and fulfill God's law regarding sexual propriety. Lust is a temptation for everyone. Some are tempted toward women, others toward men, but every person experiences the temptation. The desire is so strong because this is the way God chose for humans to procreate and populate the world. For that to happen, there is a strong desire that is innate in all human beings. We all possess it. To deny it is simply to deny reality. It is one of those temptations that usually lasts a lifetime.

Sexual nature is God-given. It is right when used within the framework and the context of the home. God created man and woman and brought them together, and He also created a method of multiplying and populating the earth. Sex is normal, natural, right, and good; in fact, it is the most beautiful expression of love between a husband and wife. From sex, children are brought into the world, and families are formed. In today's world, with its promiscuity and radicalism, every effort is made to destroy the family bond. People are mating with anyone. Children are considered disposable. As a result, the home that God intended to be the nucleus of society is weakened, and people are unwilling to experience what God intended.

In 1 John 2:15–17 we read, "Do not love the world or the things in the world. If anyone loves the world, the love of the Father is not in him. For all that is in the world — the desires of the flesh and the desires of the eyes and the pride of life — is not from the Father but is from the world. And the world is passing away along with its desires, but whoever does the will of God abides forever." These are the three ways we are tempted, the same ways Adam and Eve were tempted, and the same ways Jesus was tempted. We should not be surprised when we are tempted to lust and engage in sexual impropriety. Our response to such temptations and how well we overcome them are key to controlling lust.

We can lust for food, money, fame, attention, or sex. The word *lust* refers to an inordinate, above the limits desire for something that we should not have at a particular time or in a particular way. As a result we must learn how to live in a world that is full of lustful stimulation, while not committing the sin of lust.

The results of adultery and fornication are always bad. There are no good adulterous relationships. The results can be divorce, disease, spiritual devastation, and separation from God — all of which cause heartache and sorrow.

The temptation to lust lasts throughout our lives. If you think this temptation gets easier or goes away as you age, you are wrong. I have visited nursing homes and counseled some residents there. Nursing home staffs will tell you that there is as much promiscuity in nursing homes as there is anywhere else. With lust, we must be alert all our lives. We must always be morally strong. This commandment gives us sexual limitations. "Therefore a man shall leave his father and his mother and hold fast to his wife, and the two shall become one flesh" (Matthew 19:5). They become one in every respect. I don't know how many times in a GriefShare® class that I help teach I have heard someone say, "My husband and I used to be one, and now I am just half a person since my husband died." That is how it is supposed to be. You are so close that you are one, and when one spouse passes away, the other feels as if they are only half.

Did you know that lust can lead to adultery, even without the sexual act itself? Jesus said, "Everyone who looks at a woman with lustful intent has already committed adultery with her in his heart" (Matthew 5:28). The consequences of heart adultery may not be as difficult as the actual act of adultery, because the actual act affects so many people, whereas adultery in the heart usually affects only the one lusting. Jesus is telling us to control our thoughts. The scribes and the Pharisees had changed God's laws on marriage, divorce, and remarriage, and adultery. It seems that from the giving of the Ten Commandments that the religious leaders started trying to modify God's law, redefining it and making it easier for people to sin without thinking of it as sin. This is why Jesus told them if they sinned in their hearts, it was sin. What they did was to take the passage that said, "Do not commit adultery," and rewrote it in their laws to say,

"Do not commit adultery with a Jew." They said this because it would dishonor a Jew, one of God's chosen people. But according to their man-made laws, you could commit adultery with a slave, or with a Gentile. They had altered God's law in such a way that adultery was common among the Jewish people, and even among the theologians and religious leaders of Jesus' day.

Jesus' command in Matthew 5:28 brings it back in line with what God intended. This Scripture applies to both men and women. If a woman looks at a man lustfully, then she is also guilty of sin. No one is exempt from this command. Jesus is saying the sin of lust is a matter of the heart. If you think, *If I had the opportunity, I would commit adultery*, then you've already committed adultery in your heart.

On another occasion, Jesus said, "Unless your righteousness surpasses that of the Pharisees and the teachers of the law, you will certainly not enter the kingdom of heaven" (Matthew 5:20). The scribes and the Pharisees thought they were the absolute height of moral and spiritual righteousness. Jesus said, however, that the people under His new covenant would need to be better than the scribes and Pharisees, who had twisted and distorted the Word of God to do whatever they wanted. It is a matter of purity, and not just following a rule. It is a matter of the attitude of the heart and mind. If you have a lustful, sensual mind, it will lead to sexual sin. But we should have a mind under the control of the Holy Spirit and knowledge from the Word of God of the consequences of sin.

It is important that we realize we live in a wicked and adulterous world. In Matthew 16:4, Jesus referred to the "evil and adulterous generation." There have always been temptations and people who give into them. Today we have the internet, a sexually charged culture, and easily accessible pornography, but it has always been hard to keep our minds pure and avoid temptation.

The story of David and Bathsheba is the quintessential example of sexual temptation and its resultant sin. Theirs is a story that has been repeated millions of times as it clearly demonstrates the progression from desire to sin. Second Samuel 11:2–5 reads, "It happened, late one afternoon, when David arose from his couch and was walking on the roof of the king's house, that he saw from the roof a woman bathing; and the woman was very beautiful. And David sent and inquired about the woman. And one said, 'Is not this Bathsheba, the daughter of Eliam, the wife of Uriah the Hittite?' So David sent messengers and took her, and she came to him, and he lay with her. (Now she had been purifying herself from her uncleanness.) Then she returned to her house. And the woman conceived, and she sent and told David, 'I am pregnant.'"

Lust begins with nothing more than a thought entering the mind. Action follows. Consequences almost inescapably ensue. The results of David and Bathsheba's adulterous relationship included lying, murder, and deep regret. David repented of his sin with Bathsheba. in fact, the entirety of Psalm 51 is David's begging God to forgive him for his sin,which resulted in a nation being neglected and David separating from God.

> We live in a world where even people who acknowledge God and Jesus as His Son accept changes in God's morality.

The act of adultery is sin, but the evil heart is spiritually just as destructive. Sin begins in the mind with a thought or a look. One must control their thoughts to be successful in overcoming lust. The scribes and the Pharisees changed God's laws again and again, but they were no different than we are today. We continue to change God's Word daily in an effort to justify our actions. Adultery is no longer considered as bad as it once was. In fact, it is accepted as long as no one is harmed. If you are having fun and finding pleasure, that is the purpose of life according to millions of hedonistic people who have no spiritual values and who live by the pragmatic law of, "If it works, it is okay." We live in a world where even people who acknowledge God and Jesus as His Son accept changes in God's morality. Theologians of our day are changing the moral laws, and the general population soon accepts it.

When I first started preaching, two men — Joseph Fletcher and Harold Cox — started the idea of the "new morality." The old morality was out-of-date, and we needed a new morality for our new, emancipated era. The new morality allowed for love (as they defined it; we would call it "lust"), for people to have multiple partners, and it began to erode the old, accepted morality. When I was young, I was not prepared for the sexual onslaught of the 1960s and the new morality, and neither were many of my friends. I was reared in the church, I went to David Lipscomb for my undergraduate degree and Harding for my graduate work, and a seminary for my doctorate degree. Yet there was no mention of morality and the sins and consequences of the lack of morality. I saw people I knew well falling prey to the teaching of "moral relativism," which simply means that morality depends on the situation, and situation ethics is what's important. A theology professor at Emory University said, "God is dead." With those words, he opened the doors to free everyone from any consequences of God's law. Not only did the Jewish scribes and Pharisees change God's Word, modifying and broadening it, but we have done the same thing in our world today.

Today, modern theology is as worthless as any morally relative concept can be. Modern theology as it is taught in many seminaries today does not teach the commandments, morals, and attitudes of the Word of God. Culture has corrupted many of those who love God and are supposedly seeking to serve Him.

Proverbs 6:32–35 teaches, "He who commits adultery lacks sense; he who does it destroys himself. He will get wounds and dishonor, and his disgrace will not be wiped away. For jealousy makes a man furious, and he will not spare when he takes revenge. He will accept no compensation; he will refuse though you multiply gifts."

When I lived in Atlanta, a deacon in the church we attended was against everything. He was referred to as the "thorn in the flesh" by others. But one day, on the front page of the *Atlanta Journal Constitution* was the headline, "Attorney Murders Wife and Girlfriend." It was this man. He had been having an affair for several years, and his wife found out. She confronted him. He killed her and his girlfriend as well.

It doesn't always end like that, but adultery always causes wounds and hurt. It is a sin of pain, heartache, and destruction. It destroys relationships. Over the years, people have told me that their sins wouldn't hurt anyone. That is a lie, and it's the same kind of lie that Satan told Eve when he tempted her to take the forbidden fruit. It's a lie when people reject biblical authority. It's a lie when people change, modify, or nullify the teaching of God's Word. We are all sinners, and we all fall short of the glory of God. We must be careful that what begins in the mind does not lead to the actual physical act of adultery. Genesis 6:5 plainly says, "The Lord saw that the wickedness of man was great in the earth, and that every intention of the thoughts of his heart was only evil continually."

God hates sexual sins because they destroy the sanctity of the home and hinder the development of the personality and the soul. Sexual sins cause our divorce courts to be filled, and children are harmed as much or more than anyone else. Thousands of children live in broken homes because of sin. Those children spend one week with mom and the next with dad. That isn't the way God intended family to be, but because of sin, it often is this way for many.

Sexual immorality in our day leads to abortion as a means of birth control, rather than understanding that life begins at conception. Sexual immorality also leads to diseases such as AIDS and other sexually transmitted diseases. As important as these consequences are, they are not as important as understanding that God has always had a plan. His plans are perfect, and He knows what is right for us. He tells us that if we submit to His will and do what He asks, everything will be better. As we sin and as we refuse to follow God's will, we find it difficult to find peace, happiness, purpose, or true love.

If someone commits adultery, are they doomed? Most, if not all of us, would agree we have committed adultery in our hearts. Is there hope? Is there any way to start over? The answer is yes! Remember Mary Magdalene? She was considered a prostitute. Remember the woman at the well? She had had five husbands, and the man with whom she was currently living was not her husband. How about the woman taken in adultery who was about to be stoned to death? Jesus stepped up and said, "Which one of you has not sinned?" The Bible says from the oldest to the youngest, they dropped their stones and walked away. Anyone who has committed adultery through the ages can be forgiven. All of these were forgiven. There may be consequences to our sin, as there were for David and Bathsheba, but those consequences pale in comparison to eternal life with God.

We repent of our sins, all of them, and put them behind us. We confess them to God. I do not believe you always need to confess adultery to your partner, because it will hurt them to the depth of their being. If you are truly repentant, truly sorry, then you should tell God. But if you have an overwhelming need to confess to your partner, be sure you do it in the right way, showing the remorse and sorrow that you should.

I am reminded of the words of the hymn "Amazing Grace." "Amazing grace, how sweet the sound, that saved a wretch like me! I once was lost but now am found, was blind but now I see." There are no sins that, if repented, cannot be forgiven by God. Your spouse may choose not to forgive you, or they may forgive but be unable to forget, but either way, it is a small price to pay to be forgiven by God.

"Go, and from now on sin no more" (John 8:11). This is what Jesus said to the woman taken in adultery, and what He says to us today when we repent and confess our sins. He forgives us, cleanses us, and heals us, saying, "Don't do it again." As we realize the sanctity of marriage and the home, we should be willing to stand up in a godless, immoral society and tell the truth about God's moral laws, trying our best to live for Him.

There are those who are the innocent victims of adulterous relationships who feel unloved and unwanted. These feelings are understandable, but we need to ask God for His help in overcoming them.

Sin is sin, whether it is adultery, fornication, gay or lesbian lifestyles; — all these are sins of the flesh and are abhorrent to God. Sin always destroys. It is never helpful, beneficial, or encouraging. The Bible says, "The wages of sin is death" (Romans 6:23).

QUESTIONS

1. Discuss whether anyone is exempt from the temptation of lust.
2. What are the primary reasons or purposes for our sexual relationships?
3. What are some things for which we lust other than sex?
4. What are some of the adverse results of adultery or fornication?
5. Discuss how the temptation to lust doesn't diminish as we grow older.
6. How can a person lust and sin without ever committing the physical act?
7. How have God's requirements concerning sexual relations been exploited over the years by church leaders and theologians?
8. Discuss ways modern immorality has affected the home.

9. What was Jesus' teaching to those who had committed adultery or were living in adultery (i.e. Mary Magdalene, the woman caught in the act of adultery)?

10. What were the consequences of David and Bathsheba's sin?

CHAPTER FIVE

The Virtue of Purity

AS WE'VE LEARNED, FOR EVERY DEADLY SIN, THERE IS AN opposite virtue, and the opposite virtue to the sin of lust is purity. *Virtue* is a word we don't hear much anymore; in fact, the word *virtue* likely isn't near the top of many people's lists as an aspiration. Scripture, however, is full of virtuous people, most notably, the virtuous woman in Proverbs 31. There are many virtuous men in the Bible as well. To be virtuous we must maintain certain qualities of life, including having certain attitudes, keeping certain values, and being of a certain character. *Virtuous* means "behavior showing a high moral standard." The results of virtue are kindness, goodness, wisdom, courage, manners, courtesy, modesty, generosity, self-control, and fairness. You may be able to add more, but these are some of the qualities recognized as virtuous, righteous, and good.

It is hard to be virtuous, living in a sewer. Yes, that sounds gross, but the world today is much like a sewer. There is contamination everywhere: in business, in government, in many elements of society.

As we walk through life, trying to be virtuous, we bump up against all the trash that surrounds us. Contamination begins to cling to us, to influence us, and causes us to make bad decisions.

If we are virtuous, we will possess the fruit of the Spirit, which is love, joy, peace, patience, kindness, goodness, faithfulness, gentleness, and self-control. All these are qualities and results of virtue. Looking around the world today, it's difficult to see many people who are concerned with being virtuous. Our world is pragmatic, and most people say, "Whatever works is okay." For them, virtue, morality, and purity do not matter. People are concerned with getting what they want the way they want it. There are no rules or regulations for them. I see this attitude every day, and I am sure you do as well. As an example, my son recently sold his house. Two days before the closing, he received a call informing him that the woman purchasing his house had forged her tax returns in the closing paperwork and, as they investigated further, had never actually filed a tax return. Even so, the loan was approved because she was single and politically connected in the area. The lender said they would rather approve the loan and take the possible foreclosure loss than go through the problems involved with claims of discrimination.

We live in a mixed-up world where honesty, integrity, and virtue are difficult to maintain. Many people take advantage of the system to get what they want.

How long can we maintain purity in a world that seems to be getting progressively worse? Not to be pessimistic, but the world is not getting better in a moral and ethical sense. The heart reveals who we are. Throughout Scripture, the heart reveals the mind: "Either make the tree good and its fruit good, or make the tree bad and its fruit bad, for the tree is known by its fruit. You brood of vipers! How can you speak good, when you are evil? For out of the abundance of the heart the mouth speaks" (Matthew 12:33, 34). Here Jesus says that we can tell by the way people behave whether they are good or evil. What we say and how we say it shows where our heart and our values lie. It shows whether we have virtue and are seeking purity. When we look around the world, we see this is not a high priority for most people.

We must be careful about the heart. Jeremiah 17:9, 10 explains, "The heart is deceitful above all things, and desperately sick; who can understand it? I the Lord search the heart and test the mind, to give every man according to his ways, according to the fruit of his deeds." The Lord knows our hearts even better than we do. We can easily deceive ourselves, justifying what we want to do even if it is wrong.

> The desire of our heart must be to do the will of God, to be like our Lord and Savior.

Christians must possess purity. Jesus said in Matthew 5:8, "Blessed are the pure in heart, for they shall see God." A person whose heart's desire is to do God's will, to be like Him as much as possible, is a person who is pure in heart. The heart is important. To do the wrong things for the right reason or the right things for the wrong reasons often trips us up. We must constantly consider not only what we do, but the motive behind it. The definition of *purity* is "freedom from things that contaminate or adulterate; complete; perfect." If something is pure, it is uncontaminated. A pure life has little contamination from the world. Although even at our best, we fail miserably, the most important factor is the desire of our heart. The desire of our heart must be to do the will of God, to be like our Lord and Savior. Sometimes we stumble and fall, but that is different than being a person who wants to take advantage of everyone and selfishly exploit others. We must constantly examine our lives, and Scripture shows us how:

> "What shall we say then? Are we to continue in sin that grace may abound? By no means! How can we who died to sin still live

> in it? Do you not know that all of us who have been baptized into Christ Jesus were baptized into his death? We were buried therefore with him by baptism into death, in order that, just as Christ was raised from the dead by the glory of the Father, we too might walk in newness of life. For if we have been united with him in a death like his, we shall certainly be united with him in a resurrection like his. We know that our old self was crucified with him in order that the body of sin might be brought to nothing, so that we would no longer be enslaved to sin" (Romans 6:1–6).

There is no perfection among humanity. The only perfect person was Jesus, which gives Him the right to be a ransom for us, to pay the price for our sins, to die, and to receive the punishment we rightly deserved. When we are baptized, our sins are washed away, and we are cleansed. When we stumble throughout our Christian life, we have our own high priest to advocate for us with the Father. We can pray for forgiveness, and if our heart is repentant, we are continually cleansed from our sins and are able to maintain a kind of purity because of God's love and Christ's sacrifice. "But if we walk in the light, as he is in the light, we have fellowship with one another, and the blood of Jesus his Son cleanses us from all sin" (1 John 1:7).

We know purity is important to God because of how it's handled in Scripture. Purity is mentioned 107 times in 98 different verses in the New Testament. It is an important subject, although it isn't easy, convenient, or even comfortable to discuss. Though difficult, we must talk about and be concerned about the purity of the heart, mind, soul, the real being, and the eternal part of us that lasts beyond our death. The following verses will help you to see the importance God places on purity of heart:

> "For the Lord sees not as man sees: man looks on the outward appearance, but the Lord looks on the heart" (1 Samuel 16:7b).

> "... you will seek the Lord your God and you will find him, if you search after him with all your heart and with all your soul" (Deuteronomy 4:29).

The heart that Jesus talks about is not the physical organ, but rather it is our soul, our mind, our decision-making process. Just as we have a physical, beating heart that pumps oxygenated blood through our bodies, we also have a spiritual heart that circulates the goodness and righteousness of God throughout our very being.

"Blessed are the pure in heart, for they shall see God" (Matthew 5:8). I've thought a lot about this passage. How are we going to see God? I know we will see God when we get to heaven. What a blessed anticipation that is! I think, though, there are ways we can see God, even here on earth by being pure in heart. Contamination — sin — separates us from God, but purity brings us closer to Him. The closer we are to God, the better view we have of Him. We can see Him in the circumstances of life. I know there have been situations in my life as I crossed paths with others where I can give no other explanation than this was a "God thing." I give Him the glory, the honor, and the praise for all those situations I have experienced. They were truly providential situations, and even though the word *providence* is not mentioned in the Word of God, certainly all it refers to is God's working in our lives, which is providential.

I know that I see God in what He has done in my life and how He has led me to certain places and certain people. I see God in my everyday provisions. I believe it when God says, "Do not be anxious about tomorrow, for tomorrow will be anxious for itself" (Matthew 6:34). We have faith and sight. Most of us prefer sight over faith. We want to know there is enough money in the bank, enough food in the refrigerator, and enough clothes in the closet so that we don't have to worry. But Jesus tells us to trust Him for everything. He will make sure we have what we need. I have a friend who most would not call a Christian, but he has taught me more about trusting God than anyone I have ever met. He literally believes and practices living in faith and trusting God every day. He is one of the hardest workers I have ever known, but his trust is wholly in God to provide for his basic needs. He is sometimes in your face and rough around the edges, but his faith is pure.

I am not opposed to earning or saving at all. When we do this, we can use the benefits to the glory of God by helping others. But we need to learn to trust God more and believe that He will take care of us if we seek purity and all the other virtues that he wants us to have. I truly believe that sometimes when things are taken away from us it can be the best thing that could happen. We may consider it to be the worst tragedy of our lives, but in the long run, it may be the best thing for us spiritually. We truly see God as He enables us to live a godly lifestyle in this evil world.

I love seeing God in others. I love the God-like qualities I see in my friends, my loved ones, and my brothers and sisters in Christ. As I see God living in others, it makes me stronger. I see God in the forgiveness of sins and the love He has for us. I cannot imagine why He would even care about me or you. What would make us lovable enough for Him to give the greatest gift ever to save us? But that is how much He loves us. He has told us He knows everything about us, even down to the number of hairs on our head. He just wants us to do what the Bible asks us to do. This is another way I know I can see God: As I read, study, and apply the Bible, I can look at the world and see that the closer I get to living the Bible's teachings, the better off humanity is. The further away from it we get, the worse off we are.

I saw on the news recently that our military is doing away with the Bible and will now have just a "book of faith" to accommodate all the many faiths in the world. In one way I can understand it, but in another way I think of it as just more evidence of how far we are drifting away from the guide, the path, the light that should direct every one of us as we walk through this life. The further away we move from God, the less we will have of purity, virtue, and everything that is good in this world.

Throughout history there have been people who wanted to purify themselves. People all over the world, especially in Asia, still have purification rituals even today. People know intuitively that they have done wrong, whether or not they are familiar with the Word of God. The purpose of these purification rituals is to make them feel "right" again.

Even in the Old Testament, there were purification rituals. In the story of Bathsheba, she was on the roof bathing as part of a purification ritual called *nidda*, where a woman purifies herself seven days after her cycle. During *nidda*, a woman cannot be with her husband at all. This ritual process requires complete immersion in water. Most Jewish families had a *mikveh*, which is the pool used for purification, and they would try to make sure it was near a spring or well for the purest water. According to Jewish law, the *mikveh* should be large enough to hold 40 *seahs* of water (about 7.7 liters or 2 U.S. gallons).

Another purification ritual in the Old Testament was the scapegoat, which was instituted under the high priest, Aaron. Aaron would take a goat and place upon it all the sins of Israel that had been committed for an entire year. He would then take the goat into the desert and release it. It would run away and eventually die, and all the sins of Israel would die with it. Baptism is a purification ritual that we practice today. It is a God-blessed way of purifying and cleansing the sins and impurities in our lives. After we become Christians, prayer is another way we can purify ourselves as we confess our sins to God and ask His forgiveness. Purification is essential for the Christian throughout our lives.

In Asia, they practice purification rituals that involve scrubbing the face and hands, sometimes to the point of damaging the skin, in an effort to rid themselves of some sort of impurity in their lives. This symbolizes the significant problem of sin in our lives. The concept is that if our face and body have been washed and look clean, then we will feel clean all over, inside and out. But the cleansing has to be inside, not just outside. It is a purification and cleansing of the soul. We don't have to worry about our outer bodies, as Peter said in 1 Peter 3:21, "Baptism, which corresponds to this, now saves you, not as a removal of dirt from the body but as an appeal to God for a good conscience, through the resurrection of Jesus Christ." When we are baptized, it is not a bath. Rather, it is a cleansing of the soul as we communicate with the blood of Jesus, which washes away our sins completely.

Acts 22:16 says, "And now why do you wait? Rise and be baptized and wash away your sins, calling on his name." Acts 8:36–38 says, "And as they were going along the road they came to some water, and the eunuch said, 'See, here is water! What prevents me from being baptized?' And he commanded the chariot to stop, and they both went down into the water, Philip and the eunuch, and he baptized him."

How do we stay pure in an impure world? You won't stay pure with pornography. You won't stay pure immodestly dressed. You won't stay pure if you associate exclusively with people of the world. You must also associate with people of God. You must have standards, morals, and values, and when you do sin, you must be repentant.

We must have a meaningful church life, making sure we associate with God's people regularly: "I was glad when they said to me, 'Let us go to the house of the Lord!'" (Psalm 122:1). "And let us consider how to stir up one another to love and good works, not neglecting to meet together, as is the habit of some, but encouraging one another, and all the more as you see the Day drawing near" (Hebrews 10:24, 25).

In addition to how we socialize, other things are important, too. We should also make sure our entertainment is free of impurities.

We need to select an occupation that allows us to maintain our Christian principles and purity. We should choose Christian friends who help us to become better people rather than dragging us down. We should choose hobbies and recreational activities that are not immoral within themselves and do not cause us to have to associate exclusively with worldly, immoral people. We cannot watch movies, play games, or look at social media or internet posts that feature sexual immorality and still maintain purity. It is difficult for us to have immoral people as close friends and maintain purity. Evil companions do corrupt good morals. Christians cannot read trashy, immoral literature and remain pure. Biblical purity is about every area of our lives. Only by staying close to the Word of God, choosing faithful Christian friends who desire to be virtuous, moral, and pure, and avoiding the trash that tries to infiltrate every part of our lives, can we achieve the goal of godly purity:

> "I appeal to you therefore, brothers, by the mercies of God, to present your bodies as a living sacrifice, holy and acceptable to God, which is your spiritual worship" (Romans 12:1). This is how we stay pure, by concentrating on God, His Word, His people, and by desiring purity in all things.

QUESTIONS

1. What are some definitions of the word *purity*?

2. Where does the concept of virtue or purity originate?

3. Why do you think virtue isn't a high priority for most people today?

4. How do our actions often reveal the intentions of our heart?

5. Discuss Romans 6:1–6 and how important it is for us to desire to be pure and sinless.

6. What is the promise of Matthew 5:8?

7. How does the desire (or lack of) for purity and ethics in our friends affect us?

8. Discuss some of the purification rituals of the Old Testament.

9. What are other purification rites that are observed throughout the world?

10. Discuss how baptism is a purification rite.

11. What are some specific things we can do to maintain purity in our lives?

12. Discuss how the encouragement of Romans 12:1 relates to maintaining God's concept of purity.

CHAPTER SIX

The Sin of Sloth

IN THIS CHAPTER WE WILL DISCUSS A SUBJECT THAT MAY BE unpopular for you or somebody you know: slothfulness. Slothfulness, or laziness (as it is called in more modern Bible versions), can be a sin because it can distract us from doing the will of God.

The Bible uses the word *sluggard* to describe someone who is unwilling to do what they know they should and are capable of doing. Slothfulness is a deadly sin. Some think it is not as bad as other sins like stealing or lying, but it is described as a sin that can destroy a person's ability to do good. It takes away one's initiative to do what God asks.

Sloth is defined as "a disinclination to action or labor." Synonyms include *sluggishness*, *laziness*, *idleness*, and *indolence*. Sloth can cause us to leave undone important, even vital, responsibilities.

Have you ever seen the animal called a sloth? I saw one at the Nashville Zoo at Grassmere. I stood there for an hour waiting for it to move, and in that hour, it never even blinked! They are called the "two-toed" sloth, and they are the slowest mammal in the world. They sleep 18 hours a day and move so slowly and eat so infrequently when they are awake that algae grows on their body. The algae is what they eat. They are so lazy that they don't hunt or forage for food! If you see one, they are usually hanging upside down by their tail. That's how they spend most of their lives. They are not a good example for any other animal or person.

The Bible makes a comparison between a sloth and a lazy person, a person who is unwilling to take care of themselves and puts forth the least possible effort in everything they do. In Proverbs 6:6–8 we read, "Go to the ant, O sluggard; consider her ways and be wise. Without having any chief, officer, or ruler, she prepares her bread in summer and gathers her food in harvest." This passage compares a slow-moving sluggard and an ant. Have you ever watched an ant going about its business? They can carry loads much greater than their own weight. They are busy all the time and never slow down. The Bible holds up the ant as a good example of work, effort, and preparation. "How long will you lie there, O sluggard? When will you arise from your sleep? A little sleep, a little slumber, a little folding of the hands to rest, and poverty will come upon you like a robber, and want like an armed man" (Proverbs 6:9–11).

People who are inclined to be lazy and do nothing usually become dependent upon others. If they don't work themselves, they must find someone who will in some way work for them, providing them what they need. We should be willing to get up and work, experiencing the joy, pleasure, and God-given responsibility of a job well done. The Bible says all humans have some talent or another. We discover that talent and use it to God's glory and honor. We serve God with our talents, we make a living with our talents, we use our talents, and we should not waste our talents by leaving them unused. If we do, the Bible judges us for that.

The Bible does not teach us that the lazy person deserves our help, our charity, our welfare, or our upkeep. In fact, it says quite the opposite. "If anyone is not willing to work, let him not eat" (2 Thessalonians 3:10). This refers to an able-bodied, mentally strong person who is simply too lazy to work. The Bible says you have no responsibility to feed that person. If they get hungry enough, they might be willing to work.

"If anyone does not provide for his relatives, and especially for members of his household, he has denied the faith and is worse than an unbeliever" (1 Timothy 5:8). We have a responsibility to ourselves, to our families, to our friends, and to others. In fact, the attitude of the Bible is that we work hard all our lives to have enough for ourselves and those we love and are responsible for and still are able to help others who are in legitimate need. There are those who do need welfare or charity. These are the very young or very old, those who are sick or afflicted in some manner who simply cannot work. We are obligated to help those people. In doing so, we fulfill the will of God. When we help the disabled, we are doing God's will.

Laziness, however, does not qualify one for charity or welfare. Early in my career, I worked for the state. My colleagues and I would visit people on welfare. We knew that knocking on most doors before 11 a.m. was a waste of time. If we could get someone to come to the door, they would be so sleepy or out of it, they would not even know what was going on. If you want to go to the welfare office when it is empty, go first thing in the morning when it opens. Laziness becomes a way of life, expecting someone else to take care of you and your responsibilities.

A term I dislike is "baby mama." I talked to a guy not long ago and he was proud of it, bragging about it, saying, "I got 11 baby mamas." He had impregnated 11 women, each of whom were being cared for by the government. He was not living with any of them because if he did, the government would cancel the benefits. If our system of government allows for someone to make more money by not working than by working, that can breed laziness. Once that attitude, or welfare mentality, takes over, it is hard to overcome.

Sometimes, though, we don't know a person's situation. We find a person in need, but we don't know anything about them. My inclination has always been to help. I may be helping them with an addiction. I may be helping them with laziness or unwillingness to work. I don't know. If I don't know, and they are hungry, injured, or hurting, then I will help them and leave it in the hands of God. However, if I know that someone can work but is unwilling to do so, then I believe the Bible teaches us that we do not have a responsibility or obligation to help that person.

Many people want to live on the efforts, work, and at the expense of others. There are those who will injure themselves to avoid having to work. What kind of able-bodied person chooses to live off the efforts, money, work, and resources of another person? There was a story in the news recently about a 30-year-old man who didn't work and was still living at home with his parents. His parents kicked him out, and he went to court and sued his parents because he thought he had a right to stay there and live off them. The judge told him to get out and get a job. I am afraid that mentality is becoming far too widespread.

Others live off their friends. I have known people who bounce from one friend to another. Usually it takes about three weeks to a month when the friend will ask them to leave because they haven't done anything, haven't contributed anything, and aren't looking for a job. Then they go to another friend. There are many situations where people will do almost anything to avoid working.

I'll remind you of 2 Thessalonians 3:10 again, "If anyone is not willing to work, let him not eat." Matthew 20:1–8 teaches us that work days come before pay days. There are those who believe that "doing nothing days" come before someone else's "pay day." We must teach the value of honorable work, because it offers a feeling of accomplishment, worth, value, and dignity. Can you imagine just lying around all day, doing absolutely nothing, and expecting someone else to take care of you? What kind of mentality is that? How does that help you or anyone else? You are not contributing to any kind of productivity except the extra productivity the person taking care of you must go through — someone else having to do for you what you are perfectly capable of doing and should be doing for yourself.

Jesus teaches us, "We must work the works of him who sent me while it is day; night is coming, when no one can work" (John 9:4). That was before electricity, but I think that it should apply for us today. My father worked a 3–11 or an 11–7 shift all his life because he could make more money for our family. He was tired all the time because he still got up early and painted houses on the side to earn extra money. There are those who do everything they can do to take care of themselves and their families. All of my siblings and myself had the opportunity to go to college because our father worked hard, made sacrifices, and was willing to do whatever needed to be done to support our family.

The main sin of the 10 virgins was not stealing, lying, murder, or adultery. It was that they did not plan to take advantage of an opportunity that came their way. The greatest opportunity of their lives was missed because they neglected to get enough oil. That's the way it is in life, I'm afraid. We don't do what needs to be done and don't use the talents we have so that when the greatest opportunity of our life comes along, we are simply unprepared.

Laziness and neglect lead to lost loves. I have counseled so many families for whom the main problem in the home was the person who was supposed to be working, earning a living, and providing for the home, was unwilling to do so. Money became a distraction, and it should not have been. They simply did not want to work. They preferred to stay home and watch TV or play video games instead of doing what God says all of us need to do to find peace, purpose, and happiness: to work. We need to have something in which we can invest ourselves and show good results from it. There are many who simply don't work. There are married people who end up divorcing because the other person doesn't want to do anything. Consider the sheer number of lost homes, lost loves, and most of all lost souls by people who are unwilling to work.

We don't always see the opportunity we should. Jesus' words in Matthew 25 should give us pause. We pass up opportunities, and I'm not always sure. Sometimes we may be tired from legitimate work, but there should always be enough to help those who legitimately, honestly need our help.

"Then he will say to those on his left, 'Depart from me, you cursed, into the eternal fire prepared for the devil and his angels. For I was hungry and you gave me no food, I was thirsty and you gave me no drink, I was a stranger and you did not welcome me, naked and you did not clothe me, sick and in prison and you did not visit me.' Then they also will answer, saying, 'Lord, when did we see you hungry or thirsty or a stranger or naked or sick or in prison, and did not minister to you?' Then he will answer them, saying, 'Truly, I say to you, as you did not do it to the least of these, you did not do it to me'" (Matthew 25:41–45). The word *least* there carries a powerful meaning. It means the least able or the least capable of doing what they needed to do for themselves. Many of them were in prison at that time because they were Christians, and Christians weren't visiting other Christians. The Scripture concludes, "And these will go away into eternal punishment, but the righteous into eternal life" (Matthew 25:46). That is frightening. Not only do we have the need and responsibility to work at a job to be able to make a living and provide for our household, but we also need to have a personal outreach, helping others in need. It takes time to do this. Some of you may be retired but are volunteering your time to help others on a regular basis. If so, I commend you for that. That is what Jesus is talking about here, I believe.

When we have our health and when we have the opportunity, we serve God and do His will as effectively as we can. We may not always see the opportunity, but we should see it. Many are hungry, thirsty, sick, afflicted, and in prison. We should take advantage of those opportunities to help others. There is the potential to be effective in some areas and neglectful in other areas. We have to constantly look inside ourselves, trying to decide if we are doing what we need to be doing. I am convinced that one of Satan's main ways of taking advantage of us is to get us to simply do nothing. We can be slothful in so many aspects of life: our Bible study, in our prayer life, in our visitation, in our church attendance, in sharing our faith with others, in the way we dress and in our conversation, slothful in our giving — all kinds of ways.

> When we have our health and when we have the opportunity, we serve God and do His will as effectively as we can.

Martin Luther, the great reformer whose efforts led to the restoration movement of the 1500s, wrote these words: "The devil had a great anniversary to which he summoned all his emissaries. They were to report the efforts of all these minions on bringing others to Satan. One said, 'I let loose wild beasts in the desert on a caravan of Christians and every one of them were killed.' The Devil said, 'So what? They were all saved, if they were Christians.' Another said, 'I drove the east wind into a ship full of Christians and it sank in the storm.' The Devil said, 'So what? If they were Christians, they were saved.' Another one of his minions said, 'For ten years I tried to get a person to just be at ease with his soul, and at last I succeeded and he is ours.' The Devil shouted and the night stars of hell sang joyfully."

The sin of slothfulness and criminal spiritual neglect has probably done as much to the population of hell as any wild sin that a person may hear about.

All Satan has to do is to convince us that we are doing enough, that the minimum is acceptable, and that in our Christianity it is more about how we feel and how we think than what we do. I have some statistics to point that out. In Christendom in general, and, I believe, even in the church today, we are succumbing to this attitude of mediocrity of service. Almost two thirds of Americans say they believe in God (Harris poll), but only 18 percent of those claiming to believe in God worship on a regular basis. Most of them may go to church once or twice a year. *I believe in God, but I don't believe enough to go worship Him, and I certainly don't believe enough to give as I should. I don't believe enough to be involved in the good works of the church.* It is easy to say, "I believe." It is harder to do the work of a believer and to become a servant. Jesus said, ". . . the Son of Man came not to be served but to serve" (Matthew 20:28). As God's people that is our mission, that is what we are about, that is who we are. We are to do the work that Jesus would do if He were here, to become His hands, His feet, His spokesmen, His ambassadors, to live the life that Jesus would want us to live and serve people any way possible.

In that same survey, 86 percent (even though only 18 percent of the people were going to church regularly) said, "We think we are pleasing God. We are in good standing with God." That's a lot of people who really don't understand what Christianity is about and how we are to work and serve the Lord.

Here is another statistic that I see in our own children, our own young people. You may see it in your children or grandchildren. Seventy-eight percent of Christians today think Christianity is more about organization than about loving God and loving each other. They feel that there is something wrong with being a part of an organized church or an organized religion. They consider organized religion unacceptable, not realizing that Jesus Himself said, "On this rock I will build my church" (Matthew 16:18). Jesus set the structure for the church, telling us how to worship and what we are to do as Christians in the church. He described the moral values and attitudes that should be in the church. It is structured, or organized, but it is God's structure. It is what God expects of each one of us as we live this Christian life.

There are those who come to church and become a part of it, but if they decide not to attend, they don't want anyone questioning them. They don't want people calling and asking, "Where were you last Sunday?" In other words, they don't want accountability. They don't want someone showing enough interest in their soul to make sure they are not sick or injured. That is the mentality of millions of people who claim to be Christians.

There are 7.6 billion people on the earth. Of those 7.6 billion, 2.3 billion claim to be Christian. That is not even most of the world's population. There are slightly fewer Muslims worldwide than there are Christians. When we come to the church, we have 2.4 million people who say they are members of the Lord's church. The question is, have we reached everybody we need to reach? Has everyone who needs to be taught been taught? Are we sharing the gospel with everyone as we can? What are we doing on a daily, weekly, monthly, or yearly basis to bring someone else to Christ? What efforts are we putting forth? It is painful for me to say this because I have to look inside and ask if I am doing enough, and my answer to that is usually "no." We all can do more. Unfortunately we are not always reaching our children, grandchildren, and great-grandchildren.

Here are more interesting statistics. Fifty-nine percent of new Christians say they came to faith through friends and family, not through preaching. Nearly 60 percent of those who describe themselves as Christians say they did so because they saw somebody else living the Christian life, being the kind of person they are supposed to be, setting an example. That is what I call personal evangelism. Sixty-four percent say they came to believe as a result of conversations with family or friends, not through listening to a preacher. I am certainly not putting down the Scripture that tells us to go into all the world and preach the gospel. Often we narrow the word *preach* too much, thinking that preaching can only be done by the preacher. Preaching should be done by all of us. Every one of us should be "preaching" as we share our faith daily with anyone who shows any inclination to listen and by modeling Christ in our lives before all others.

All of us fail doing what we should and living as we should live. We need to keep trying, doing as much as we possibly can. We will be judged as Christians according to Matthew 25, not on just whether we have been baptized, but also on our actions. I think that is why sometimes we play up the plan of salvation and play down the work of the Christian. I can say anytime, anywhere that I have repented, confessed, and been baptized, and that I study my Bible. I cannot, however, always say that I am out feeding those who need to be fed, giving water to those who are thirsty, or visiting the sick and those in prison. Jesus said that is the criteria by which we will be judged.

We've already studied *pride*, which is kind of opposite of sloth or laziness. Laziness, or slothfulness, says I am not even going to do what humans are supposed to do. I am not going to do anything at all. I will sleep my life away, wasting every minute of the time that God has given me. One elevates a person to God, and the other dehumanizes a person. Both are wrong, and both can lead to destruction.

In the parable of the talents, we note that there was a reward and a punishment. One of the people in that parable was called "slothful." That was the person who had one talent and went out and buried it, not doing anything with it. He did not lose it, but he didn't use it. When the Lord came back, he still had it, but it had never been used.

The person who had five talents had taken those talents, used them, and made five more. Sometimes we are afraid to use our talents for one reason or another, so we bury them, denying we have them and refusing to use them. That does no one any good. *There is someone in your life who needs the talent that you have,* and your unwillingness to use that talent to the glory and honor of God is neglecting in some way to bless the life of a friend, family member, or even a stranger.

But it doesn't have to be that way. Be excited and glad to produce, help, and be useful to God and to one another. Do whatever you can whenever you can to be a positive influence on the world and a servant of God. If we do that, we will be blessed.

One Final Thought

Whatever the motive, our current political climate rewards people for not working. Able-bodied individuals are paid to not work. This current governmental policy is detrimental in many ways. Most importantly, it keeps people from using their God-given talents and experiencing and enjoying the affirmation of doing a job well and producing goods or services that are beneficial to humanity.

Another dangerous trend in our current society is that our young people are preoccupied with sedentary activities — playing computer games or spending time on social media. They are not getting exercise and perhaps not learning the value of work and skills. Three generations ago, most young people, when they reached the age of about 13–15, were performing some sort of tasks and receiving allowances for work done. Today, most of our time is occupied with non-physical activities, leading to obesity and, in many instances, to laziness. We need to encourage our young people to be outside more, working and playing in activities that give them exercise, which strengthens the body as well as the mind.

QUESTIONS

1. What is "sloth"? How is it defined?

2. What are the characteristics of the animal called a sloth?

3. What is the biblical comparison between a sloth and a lazy person?

4. Discuss 1 Timothy 5:8.

5. Discuss whether you believe that if an able-bodied person is unwilling to work that they should not be fed (2 Thessalonians 3:10)?

6. What was the main tragedy of the 10 virgins parable in Matthew 25:1–13?

7. How does one person's unwillingness to work affect the love and respect of other members of the family?

8. Do you feel we are working as hard as we should to spread the gospel to the entire world? Why or why not?

9. How does our current cultural climate affect our attitude toward work?

10. What were Adam and Eve's responsibilities for working?

11. How is rest essential to God's plan for useful work?

12. Discuss the work problem for the church in Thessalonica.

CHAPTER SEVEN

The Virtue of Work

IN THE LAST CHAPTER, WE STUDIED SLOTH, OR LAZINESS. Laziness is destructive in almost every way — mentally, physically, and spiritually. Mentally, laziness leads to mental disorders and irrational thinking. Physically, laziness leads to a sedentary lifestyle, which can, in turn, lead to obesity and over 40 other chronic diseases, including heart disease, type 2 diabetes, dementia, and some cancers. One study even shows that for every week you are sedentary, it is the equivalent of smoking a pack of cigarettes. Spiritually, laziness denies God's plan for us to work. It separates us from God because we refuse one of the basic responsibilities of mankind.

Many famous philosophers and doctors have spoken to the value of being active. Hippocrates, the father of modern medicine, said, "Work or activity is the elixir of life." We were created and designed to work.

God, Our Perfect Example

We are created in the image of God, and God works. Read Genesis 1:1–27 and see how He worked. After each part of God's creation, He states, "It is good." Work should be good. It should be beneficial and helpful, bringing us a sense of accomplishment as it did for God. In creating the world and everything in it and beyond it, God was working, putting forth effort. Having been created in the image of God, we can certainly do no less.

> As we work in our occupations, our work must be good, moral, and virtuous. We must use our effort, our work, to the glory of God and the benefit of mankind.

In the beginning, Adam and Eve were put in the garden and told to tend it. They were given this responsibility because it is important for man to work. Think of the chaos there would be in the world if no one worked, if no one did anything except just lie around and try to stay alive. It would not be a pleasant place to exist if that were the case. God continues to work, even today. He sustains the world and everything in it. He answers the prayers and requests of His children everywhere. He supervises heaven and everything in it. He provides for each one of His children through the Holy Spirit, and our thoughts are communicated to Him through God's Spirit and our Savior, Jesus. After the initial creation, God saw His work, and everything was good.

As we work in our occupations, our work must be good, moral, and virtuous. We must use our effort, our work, to the glory of God and the benefit of mankind. "The Lord God took the man and put him in the garden of Eden *to work it and keep it*" (Genesis 2:15, emphasis added). As we make our place in the world, there is a job designed specifically for our abilities, talents, and resources. There is something that we especially, gifted by God, can do. Just as God the Father is a perfect example for us in our lives, so Jesus, His Son and our Savior, is also a perfect example. Jesus worked all His adult life. In some way or another, He was busy and active, preparing for His main mission of the salvation of humanity. Jesus only preached for three years. He was probably a carpenter for 18–20 years of His life. But even as a young man, possibly age 12–14, He realized that He must be about the business of His Father. Even then, He was studying and preparing for the greatest mission and work of His life. Doing God's will was always His ultimate desire, no matter the challenge. His first question, and always His ultimate answer is, "Not my will, by thy will be done." This should be our view as well. Whatever we do in life, whatever occupation we pursue, it should always be in doing God's will in one way or another.

Jesus' work was service. He came not to be served, but to serve. In some way, everything we do as human beings is either serving others or producing a commodity valuable to humanity. Jesus' service was the greatest of all. He helped people in every way. He gave them spiritual advice and encouragement. He healed their bodies and even raised the dead. He taught His disciples and apostles a perfect way of life, and it is recorded for us to imitate. He was always busy doing good for others and accomplishing His God-given purpose in life.

"Bondservants, obey your earthly masters with fear and trembling, with a sincere heart, as you would Christ, not by the way of eye-service, as people-pleasers, but as bondservants of Christ, doing the will of God from the heart, rendering service with a good will as to the Lord and not to man, knowing that whatever good anyone does, this he will receive back from the Lord, whether he is a bondservant or is free. Masters, do the same to them, and stop your threatening, knowing that he who is both their Master and yours is in heaven, and that there is no partiality with him" (Ephesians 6:5–9). Here Paul is encouraging everyone to do the work they are assigned or have chosen. He uses the most extreme example of slavery or bondage and says even then, even under duress and restraint, we should do our best at what we are assigned or required to do, not trying just to please men when they are watching but even doing it "as unto the Lord."

Any honest, virtuous work has its own dignity and should be respected. I do not believe Paul was giving an opinion on the rightness or wrongness of slavery. I personally think slavery is abhorrent, but that is not the point of Paul's example. He is simply saying that no matter what the circumstances of our life may be, we should use our talents, abilities, and opportunities to the glory of God, working not to please men, but to please Him.

Joseph was a slave, yet because of his faithfulness to his own responsibilities and obligations, he rose to become second in command of Egypt. Any promotion or advancement we receive should be because we have done the best job possible, making us eligible to move up to more challenging responsibilities with more compensation. The dignity of work can be seen first in God and then in Jesus. Today, it can certainly be seen in God's people as they morally and ethically perform their responsibilities and jobs, contributing positively and beneficially to the needs of others.

Rest

Work is necessary and essential; so is rest. The Bible says God rested after His work. "Thus the heavens and the earth were finished, and all the host of them. And on the seventh day God *finished his work* that he had done, and he *rested* on the seventh day from all his work that he had done. So God blessed the seventh day and made it holy, because on it God *rested* from all his work that he had done in creation" (Genesis 2:1–3, emphasis added).

If we work hard at our job responsibilities, then we will certainly need to rest. Rest is essential to a good life and a good work. God's law under Moses was, "You work six days, and then you rest on the seventh." Under the Old Testament law, He made the seventh day holy. He gave restrictions as to how far a person could travel, and the kind of effort they could put forth on the Sabbath, even restricting them from cooking, instructing them to prepare their meals the day before. God, who made us, understands that we need a day of rest, meditation, reflection, and recreation.

If God rested after His work, we certainly need to rest after ours. Jesus needed to rest as He went about His ministry. In Mark 4:35–40, we read of an incident where Jesus had been working, teaching, healing, and performing miracles, and He was exhausted. Jesus and some of the crowd took boats and were going to the other side of the sea. A terrible storm arose, and the disciples became afraid. Jesus performed another miracle in bringing about peace and calm to the sea. Notice afterward that Jesus went back to sleep after He calmed the storm. If we do what we are designed to do for our jobs and responsibilities, if we perform them well, we are going to need to rest. It doesn't matter how noble the work may be, we must rest.

Some involved in spiritual work can pour themselves into it so much that they refuse to get necessary rest. It then becomes detrimental to them physically, mentally, and spiritually. I had a good friend several years ago who did personal work, teaching people individually, and he did it seven days a week. In fact, I would often help him during the week. We would sometimes knock on doors at 8 or 8:30 at night, and I was often afraid we would be met at the door with a gun! But most of the time, people were welcoming. My friend, though, never slowed down. In doing this good work, he neglected his family as well as his own personal health, and as a result, he died at only 45 years old of a massive heart attack.

Doing God's work does not mean we ignore God's teachings and requirements. Just as there are those who work too much and too often, refusing to rest, there are others who refuse to work at all. This was one of the problems in the church at Thessalonica. Some refused to work, simply living off others in the church who were working and producing. "Now we command you, brothers, in the name of our Lord Jesus Christ, that you keep away from any brother who is walking in idleness and not in accord with the tradition you received from us. For you yourselves know how you ought to imitate us, because we were not idle when we were with you, nor did we eat anyone's bread without paying for it, but with toil and labor we worked night and day, that we might not be a burden to any of you. It was not because we do not have that right, but to give you in ourselves an example to imitate," (2 Thessalonians 3:6–9). Here Paul says to not have anything to do with those who are idle and refuse to work.

There seem to have been some who came to the church at Thessalonica for a free ride, refusing to do their part in providing for their own necessities. Paul reminds us in this passage that he always worked and provided for his own needs. He paid his own way for his food and other necessities. Paul supported himself by being a tentmaker. He worked hard, laboring day and night, making sacrifices, probably not getting enough rest. His desire to serve the Lord and share the gospel with others was always a heavy burden and his major motivation. Paul here in Thessalonians goes so far as to say in verse 10, "If anyone is not willing to work, let him not eat." We must be willing to work to be able to receive the blessings of the church and of God.

So two major, essential requirements for us are that we work, using the talents and blessings God has given us, and that we rest from our work. Exodus 20:9–10 says, "Six days you shall labor, and do all your work, but the seventh day is a Sabbath to the LORD your God. On it you shall not do any work...."

The Moral Requirements of Work

Many people work hard at criminal enterprises or immoral occupations. Just working hard is not enough. It must be working at something that is moral, virtuous, righteous, and acceptable to God. Even when it is a good work, some feel their work is more valuable or important than anyone else's. They take pride in who they are and what they do. They believe the title they wear gives them certain eminence and respectability. Just as the Pharisee and publican were praying, the Pharisee indicated his superior attitude toward all he did and his disdain for what the publican did, thanking God that he, in effect, was better than others because of who he was. We should have respect for everyone's work if it is virtuous, noble, and righteous. We should never look down on anyone because of the occupation they hold, but should be thankful that there are people who are willing, capable, talented, and gifted in doing all that needs to be done in our world.

We need to avoid the danger of believing the compensation we receive from our work is the gauge for the importance of that work. There are many necessary, important jobs that do not carry with them high compensation. I have the utmost respect for teachers, who certainly are not paid for the value of their work. We know that wealth is not an indication of the importance of a work, especially to God. There is nothing wrong with being wealthy and making a lot of money, provided it is made honorably and used wisely. Job, Abraham, Joseph, Jacob, Solomon, and many others in the Bible were wealthy people, but we should not judge the worth of a position or job simply by the amount of money attached to its efforts, and we should be thankful that there are those who are willing to work at jobs that might pay less but are essential to public education, public safety, and to national security. We should be careful not to allow greed to become a motivation for what we do. It is true that greed is just as much a temptation for the poor as it is for the rich, and that anyone in any position or job can be greedy.

Finally, remember that your true identity is not just what you do, but who you are. Your job does not completely identify you. Who you are as a person and the qualities and virtues of your life identify who you are more than the work you may do. These qualities and virtues go with you everywhere, whether at work, social events, religious services, or just spending time with friends. Everything we do should be done to the glory of God. We should do it as if it is for God. That requires us to always do our best in every good work.

QUESTIONS

1. What are some physical problems associated with the unwillingness to work?

2. Discuss what God did in terms of creating man and everything on the earth and in the sea. How is God our perfect example in demonstrating work?

3. What were Adam and Eve's work responsibilities?

4. How is Jesus our perfect example in fulfilling the responsibility of work and service?

5. How did Joseph demonstrate the dignity and the rewards of good work?

6. How is rest necessary and essential?

7. What did God do when He finished His creation work?

8. What are the moral requirements associated with legitimate work?

9. Discuss whether our identity is completely associated with our work.

CHAPTER EIGHT

The Sin of Greed

ECCLESIASTES 5:10 SAYS, "HE WHO LOVES MONEY WILL NOT be satisfied with money, nor he who loves wealth with his income; this also is vanity." Just two verses later we read, "The full stomach of the rich will not let him sleep," (Ecclesiastes 5:12). The love of money can never be satisfied. Trying to get more, do more, own more, are all like grasping at the wind, as Solomon says in Ecclesiastes 1. When we look at our own lives, we often find that we spend much of our time trying to accumulate wealth. It is fine to do that, because there are rich people who are not greedy and who are doing an incredible amount of good with their wealth. A.M. Burton, founder of Life and Casualty Insurance Company in Nashville, Tennessee, gave away 90 percent of his income and lived on only 10 percent during much of his life. The 90 percent was millions and millions of dollars, and the 10 percent was a lot of money, too. But the point is, he gave away the majority of his money.

He did not allow his money to possess him; rather, he possessed it and used it to the glory of God.

Often, people do not start out to just make money or become rich. Greed isn't even a thought. In fact, some of the people who do the most good in this world are those who start out with an "I just want to help" attitude. As a result, they are financially blessed and are able to do much good for others.

I know it is not always good to use personal experiences, but I admire a local philanthropic couple as much as anyone else I know. I don't think they started out to make a lot of money, but one of them had a good idea, and sometimes that is all it takes in this world. That good idea blessed so many people and continues to do so. Having money is not what is most important. Money can do good things. Money can send missionaries, build hospitals, help orphans and widows. Money is neutral. It is how we feel about money, what it means to us, and whether we are willing to allow the money we are blessed with to be used to the glory of God.

Riches are a snare in so many ways. Many who are greedy and covetous have been led to commit all kinds of sins. Over the years I have known a few wealthy people. One was Cecil Day, who formed Days Inn of America. Every time I met with Cecil, he would start with a prayer and Scripture reading. He said, "I want to build this company for one reason — I want families to be able to travel and stay together, but not have to go into debt to travel." He became highly successful with his chain of motels. His intentions were not to become wealthy, but to help others. The motive behind our actions is important.

Greed has some siblings: covetousness, avarice, and selfishness. Greed is a selfish frame of mind and mentality. It says "I want more and more and more." Andrew Carnegie was once asked, "How much money is enough?" His reply? "Just a little bit more." A greedy person can never get enough. No matter how much you accumulate, if your heart and your mind are not right, and God is not the center of your life, then what you have will possess you.

Greed is never satisfied. It makes necessities of luxury, opulence, and abundance. We think we cannot live without things, but, if we were not so entangled in our love of money and things, we could live much happier lives. Who isn't familiar with this admonition from 1 Timothy? "The love of money is a root of all kinds of evils" (6:10). For a little bit of money, people will steal, kill, sell their bodies, and do all kinds of repulsive things. There are people who literally sell their souls for more money. Does our money have us, or do we have our money?

Continuing in 1 Timothy 6:10, we read, "For the love of money is a root of all kinds of evils. It is through this craving that some have wandered away from the faith and pierced themselves with many pangs." If wealth could buy happiness, then all the movie stars, singers, and sports figures would be the happiest people on earth, but they are not. In fact, there are many poor people who are happy and content. *Contentment* is a word many of us have lost sight of. It means we are happy, or satisfied, with where we are and with what God has allowed us to have. Do we have our money, or does our money have us?

There are many biblical examples of greed. Remember the rich young ruler who came to Jesus? "And behold, a man came up to him, saying, 'Teacher, what good deed must I do to have eternal life?' And he said to him, 'Why do you ask me about what is good? There is only one who is good. If you would enter life, keep the commandments.' He said to him, 'Which ones?' And Jesus said, 'You shall not murder, You shall not commit adultery, You shall not steal, You shall not bear false witness, Honor your father and mother, and, You shall love your neighbor as yourself.' The young man said to him, 'All these I have kept. What do I still lack?' Jesus said to him, 'If you would be perfect, go, sell what you possess and give to the poor, and you will have treasure in heaven; and come, follow me.' When the young man heard this, he went away sorrowful, for he had great possessions" (Matthew 19:16–22). Jesus could see into the heart of this young man, and He saw the one thing that separated him from God: his love of money. It wasn't the fact that he had money; it was the fact that he thought more of it than he should have.

What we love, we serve. The love of money is the root of all kinds of evil. What do we love? What is most important in our lives? It is a fact of life that we must have money to live. We need food, shelter, and clothing, and God says we are to work and earn a living to purchase all these things and have enough left over to help the poor. That is what each of us should strive to do.

Money can be such a blessing for so many, but it can also be a curse. "But those who desire to be rich fall into temptation, into a snare, into many senseless and harmful desires that plunge people into ruin and destruction" (1 Timothy 6:9). We read in 1 Kings 21 of King Ahab and Naboth. Naboth had a small vineyard, and the king wanted it. He offered to buy it from Naboth, but Naboth did not want to sell it. Ahab complained to his wife, Jezebel, saying "I want Naboth's vineyard, but he won't sell it to me." Jezebel replied, "Don't worry, I will take care of it." Then Jezebel began to plot. She spread a rumor that Naboth had blasphemed God and was a traitor to the kingdom. He was stoned to death for these "crimes," and Ahab took possession of the vineyard he had coveted.

The love of money is the root of all kinds of evil and sin. It causes people to do things that they would not do otherwise. It becomes a god to them, and that is the problem with greed. Greed replaces God. If you have all you need or want, you may not need God. God knows what our needs are, and He will supply all our needs, but if we have a platinum credit card or a second mortgage to buy whatever we want, we need God less. Shopping centers have become our cathedrals, where we overindulge in buying things to make ourselves happy, when things alone will never make us happy. Remember Barnabas, the encourager? He sold a piece of land and gave the money to the church. The church recognized this gift as helpful to the kingdom of God. Ananias and Sapphira liked the praise Barnabas received, and they sold a piece of their land. They kept part of the proceeds for themselves and gave the rest to the apostles. However, they lied and told the apostles that they were giving all the money they received from the sale of their land. Their greed caused them to lie, and as a result, they both died (Acts 5-1:11)! Barnabas trusted God enough to give all the money he made from selling his land, but Ananias and Sapphira could not bring themselves to do that.

We must be careful in in the United States because greed is almost a way of life. It is often encouraged. We want to do the best we can, to possess as much as we can, because, unfortunately, that is how success is defined and someone's worth is measured. But that is not God's way. "For what does it profit a man to gain the whole world and forfeit his soul?" (Mark 8:36).

Remember Joseph's brothers? They were jealous of Joseph, but that jealousy quickly turned to greed when they saw the caravan coming. They sold Joseph, their own brother, into slavery. Slavery has almost always throughout history been the result of greed, but ultimately the person most enslaved is the one who is greedy.

There are people who have highly successful businesses, but who treat their employees terribly. They don't share their blessings with others. In Luke 12 we read of the rich farmer: "Someone in the crowd said to him, 'Teacher, tell my brother to divide the inheritance with me.' But he said to him, 'Man, who made me a judge or arbitrator over you?'" (Luke 12:13, 14). Today, when someone dies, the children immediately start complaining and arguing over who is going to get what. Their greed takes over. I know of a situation in which the children were literally pushing and shoving each other in the kitchen over who was going to get the canned goods in the pantry. It is amazing how greed affects us.

Continuing in Luke 12 we read, "And he said to them, 'Take care, and be on your guard against all covetousness, for one's life does not consist in the abundance of his possessions.' And he told them a parable, saying, 'The land of a rich man produced plentifully, and he thought to himself, "What shall I do, for I have nowhere to store my crops?" And he said, "I will do this: I will tear down my barns and build larger ones, and there I will store all my grain and my goods. And I will say to my soul, 'Soul, you have ample goods laid up for many years; relax, eat, drink, be merry.'" But God said to him, "Fool! This night your soul is required of you, and the things you have prepared, whose will they be?" So is the one who lays up treasure for himself and is not rich toward God'" (Luke 12:15–21).

How many times have we seen that happen? People work all their lives, get to the point that they can really enjoy life, and then they die. The entirety of Ecclesiastes speaks to this problem. The possessions are left to people who don't know the worth of them and never been invested in them, and they end up fighting over them. People become greedy, and their hearts become tarnished.

Judas is probably one of the saddest examples in the Bible. He knew Jesus as well as anyone, associated with Him, and heard all His teachings. Yet greed entered his heart, and Judas sold Jesus for 30 pieces of silver. What he realized though, having known Jesus, was that he could not live without Him. Judas tried to undo the betrayal, but it was not possible, and he ultimately took his own life.

Greed is so deceptive. We think if we can just have this or that, then we will be happy. When I was counseling, I had one lady who would say each time she came in, "All I want is a swimming pool. Why can't my husband give me a swimming pool? All my friends have swimming pools, and I want a swimming pool!" This went on for over a year, and she finally got a swimming pool. It wasn't three months after that until she decided she needed a tennis court to be happy. That's the way we are. If we put our happiness and our peace of mind in things, thinking things will bring us what we are desire, then we will never be satisfied. That hole in your heart can only be filled with a relationship with God. We should do all we possibly can to take everything God blesses us with and use it to His glory and honor, giving Him the praise for everything accomplished.

The prodigal son went to his father, saying, "Give me what is mine." The father had not yet died, but the son didn't want to wait. The father gave his son his portion of the inheritance, and the son wasted all of it. That is often what people do when they inherit lots of money early in life. But when the son went from "Father, *give* me" to "Father, *forgive* me," he found what he was really seeking. The money from his father did not give the son what he wanted. But when it was all gone, and he was reduced to eating the pigs' food, he came to himself and said, "Father, forgive me." I hope when we come to that point in our lives when we realize we are going down the wrong road, that we can come to our senses and say, "Father, forgive me," and turn and go home to the Father.

Greed, idolatry, money — all these things, in many instances, are an attempt to replace God. If we have everything we want, we can buy everything we don't need. In having all the pleasures that we really shouldn't have, and really don't need, we attempt to replace God. That is the whole idea of greed. It is an attempt to live life as we want to live it, on our terms and with our wrong values and goals, instead of God's.

Jesus taught the parable of the sower and the seed. The seed fell on various types of ground, and this is what Jesus said concerning the seed that fell among thorns: "As for what was sown among thorns, this is the one who hears the word, but the cares of the world and the *deceitfulness of riches* choke the word, and it proves unfruitful" (Matthew 13:22, emphasis added). The seed is sown, the Word is taught, but we are possessed with wanting more and more, and it leads us away from God the Father. Money becomes our God, things become our first love, and we are simply unable to live the kind of life God wants us to live.

Greed keeps us from depending on God. Euripides said, "If you want to make a man happy, do not add to his possessions, but subtract from his desires." It is called contentment. Often, we want more than we need, and that is what causes the problem. Happiness is often where we least expect to find it, in being content with what God has blessed us.

Steve Jobs, the late CEO of Apple, Inc. said, "I reached the pinnacle of success in business, and in others' eyes my life was the epitome of success. However, aside from my work, I had little joy. In the end, wealth is only a fact that I am all too well accustomed to. At this moment, lying on my sickbed and recalling my whole life, I realize that wealth that I took so much pride in has paled in comparison to the meaninglessness of my life as I face my impending death." He passed away less than a week later. He thought he had everything it took to be happy, but he would have given everything he had to be healed.

Other rich men have said the same thing. John D. Rockefeller said, "I have many millions, but they have brought me no happiness at all. The poorest man I know is the man who has nothing but money." Cornelius Vanderbilt said, "The care of millions of dollars is just too great a burden. There is no pleasure in it for me." John J. Astor described himself as "the most miserable man on the face of the earth." But the Bible says giving is the answer for greed. Give, don't hoard or collect. In giving, we find more happiness than in receiving. "It is more blessed to give than to receive" (Acts 20:35).

> "'Therefore I tell you, do not be anxious about your life, what you will eat or what you will drink, nor about your body, what you

will put on. Is not life more than food, and the body more than clothing? Look at the birds of the air: they neither sow nor reap nor gather into barns, and yet your heavenly Father feeds them. Are you not of more value than they? And which of you by being anxious can add a single hour to his span of life? And why are you anxious about clothing? Consider the lilies of the field, how they grow: they neither toil nor spin, yet I tell you, even Solomon in all his glory was not arrayed like one of these. But if God so clothes the grass of the field, which today is alive and tomorrow is thrown into the oven, will he not much more clothe you, O you of little faith? Therefore do not be anxious, saying, "What shall we eat?" or "What shall we drink?" or "What shall we wear?" For the Gentiles seek after all these things, and your heavenly Father knows that you need them all. But seek first the kingdom of God and his righteousness, and all these things will be added to you'" (Matthew 6:25–33).

> We will never find true happiness, peace, and purpose in doing things our own way, but only in doing them God's way.

The Difference

What is the difference? The difference is knowing that what you accumulate isn't actually yours at all. It all belongs to God. Remember the rich farmer with his barns and his crops that were actually just on loan from God? Here Jesus says we will have all we need if we follow Him. Do you believe that? Do you believe that if you are doing the right thing that God will take care of you? I pray you do, because that is what Scripture says. We are God's children, and He wants to give His children the best. God wants us to understand that He has provided for us the best way of life, even from the beginning. He gave Adam and Eve everything they needed. It is only when we choose to go in another direction that we really begin to disappoint God and ourselves. We will never find true happiness, peace, and purpose in doing things our own way, but only in doing them God's way.

"As for those who are rich in this present age, charge them not to be haughty, nor to set their hopes on the uncertainty of riches, but on God, who richly provides us with everything to enjoy" (1 Timothy 6:17). If you are rich, do not depend on those riches. They are uncertain. If we are in God's will, living for Him and serving Him, we will be taken care of. He will provide for us. And the more we give of what we have, the more God will bless us. It is about responsibility and using the talents and abilities with which we have been blessed to God's glory and honor.

What we can touch, see, and possess will never make us complete or fulfill our destiny and purpose. True happiness comes from doing the will of God. Who or what we love is what we serve — God or money. God wants us to depend on Him. If we are His children, no doubt He will take care of us. Does what we supposedly have or own bring us closer to God or cause us to love and trust him less? Greed and covetousness are idolatry. These are deadly sins.

QUESTIONS

1. How is the love of money the root of all kinds of evil?

2. How is the motive behind our efforts to earn a living or to create wealth an indication of whether it is greed or not?

3. How is money neutral, neither good nor bad?

4. What are some biblical examples of people being greedy?

5. Discuss 1 Timothy 6:9.

6. How many sins were involved in Ahab and Jezebel's taking of Naboth's vineyard?

7. Why is greed sometimes the result of pride, as in the case of Ananias and Sapphira?

8. Discuss Luke 12:15–21.

9. Discuss the motives for Judas' betrayal of the Lord. What does his background as keeper of the purse tell us?

10. How was the prodigal son greedy?

CHAPTER NINE

The Virtue of Generosity

IN THE PREVIOUS CHAPTER, WE STUDIED GREED, WHICH causes people to do things that they would never consider if their hearts and minds were right. Greed infiltrates us, expanding and taking over our lives. It causes us to become people whom God cannot use. For every deadly sin, there is a life-giving virtue that counteracts that sin. A virtue that, if we adopt it in our lives, will make us better people, overcoming the deadly sins.

The opposite of greed is generosity — charity, giving, sacrificing. The importance of generosity cannot be overstated, because "God loves a cheerful giver" (2 Corinthians 9:7). God loves a person who is willing to make sacrifices, giving up something they value or want to help someone else. God values that, and He loves people who are generous. As we look through the Bible, there is no doubt that generosity is a powerful, motivating quality of life.

Over 2,300 verses in the Bible are dedicated to giving, charity, or generosity. One third of all the parables Jesus taught were about generosity and giving. It is something that is important to God and a quality He wants His people to possess. Generosity is the only answer to greed. As we look at generosity, I hope that we can examine our own lives, knowing that God wants us to be generous.

God created Adam and Eve in His image and gave them godly characteristics. God wanted the best for them, so He placed them in a paradise, giving them everything they could possibly want or need. They had purpose, they worked, they knew what contentment was, and they knew no sin. He gave them the ability to be happy and peaceful, and that's what we're seeking. God did not create robots. He gave us free will and choice. He wants us to do what we do because we believe Him when He tells us what is best for us, what will bring us happiness, purpose, and peace.

God's antagonist, Satan, the father of all lies, tries to convince us that God is wrong and that he is right. He lied to Adam and Eve and brought about the fall of mankind. We repeat that fall every time we choose to do wrong, and we suffer the same consequences. We are separated from God, and we die physically at some point in time. Yet God wants to bring us back to Him. He wants us to be in the proper relationship with Him. He wants us to be able to pray to Him as a child speaks to their father, telling Him our needs. He, in turn, will answer and bless us. God paid the price to buy us back, and in doing so, gave us the most generous, priceless gift He is capable of giving. "For God so loved the world" — every one of us — that He gave His best, not what was left over, not some meaningless patchwork, but the best He had: His own Son. God sent Jesus Christ to live among us to show us how to live. Simply living a perfect example, though, was not enough. That perfect person, the Son of God, had to die to take on our sins and satisfy the justice of God.

God's mercy and grace satisfied His justice. We can do no less. If we are not inspired by all that God has done and is doing for us, we cannot be inspired to be the right kind of people. God generously gave the best He had. Do we give our best to Him in return? Do we give the best of our time, our talents, our money? Or do we give Him the leftovers, what we really don't need? I pray earnestly that we will learn the lesson that true love always gives its best. True love always sacrifices, always becomes invested, not acting as a spectator or bystander but completely involved. We invest all we have and all we are into God and one another. That is who we are as God's people. For this reason, great rewards and great dividends will come to us.

> God generously gave the best He had.
> Do we give our best to Him in return?

I love the all-inclusive, descriptive statement that says, "God is love." Do you want to know what God is like? He is love. Every facet, every nuance is love. That it His entire being. He wants the best for us, giving us the perfect example of Jesus and a compass in the form of His Word, He has done everything possible to make us all we can be, should be, and need to be here on earth and to spend eternity with Him in heaven.

The word *love* is interchangeable with the word *charity*. If you are charitable, you love, and if you love, you will give and be charitable. We have faith, hope, and love, but the greatest of these is love, because it affects more here on this earth, and it is parat of what will get us to heaven — doing the will of God and loving Him.

God's generous and giving spirit is shown in His people. God teaches us by example and by commandment. What God possesses perfectly, we try to imitate and make a part of our lives, and to the extent we do so, we become like Him. We are not perfect like He is, but we should imitate His perfect qualities.

In Genesis 37, we read that Joseph started out chosen by God with special talents and abilities. He had the ability to interpret dreams and had been doing so from an early age. His brothers became jealous and planned to kill him. Instead, their greed took over when they saw a slave-trading caravan, and they sold their brother into slavery. If our hearts are right, and we are using the talents God has blessed upon us, regardless of the jealousy of anyone, God will continue to be with us. As long as we are doing what we are supposed to do, God will bless us, no matter the circumstances.

Joseph went to Egypt and served in Potiphar's house, and he showed his abilities and integrity to the point of being put in charge of the entire household. Potiphar's wife lied about Joseph, though he had done nothing wrong, and he was imprisoned. But even in prison Joseph excelled and eventually had the opportunity to interpret Pharaoh's dreams. As a result, Joseph was elevated to the second position in Egypt. He maintained his integrity, his love for the Lord, and his value to the Lord all his life. Nothing dissuaded him. He could have become discouraged and given up when he was sold into slavery or when he was falsely accused and imprisoned, but he did not. He kept serving God regardless of what others did to him.

Eventually he had the opportunity for the greatest generosity of all. His brothers came to him, asking for food as their land was suffering from famine. He could have been resentful and punished his brothers for their mistreatment of him. But Joseph, displaying the qualities of God, was generous, sending his brothers home with all the food they needed. He forgave his brothers and provided for their needs.

Generosity elicits forgiveness, and forgiveness elicits generosity. If we can learn to be forgiving and generous, we will be more like God. Joseph was a generous person. I don't know that any of us, having gone through the same circumstances, would have acted in the same manner, but we should.

In Luke 10:30-36 we read, "A man was going down from Jerusalem to Jericho, and he fell among robbers, who stripped him and beat him and departed, leaving him half dead. Now by chance a priest was going down that road, and when he saw him, he passed by on the other side. So likewise a Levite, when he came to the place and saw him, passed by on the other side. But a Samaritan, as he journeyed, came to where he was, and when he saw him, he had compassion. He went to him and bound up his wounds, pouring on oil and wine. Then he set him on his own animal and brought him to an inn and took care of him. And the next day he took out two denarii and gave them to the innkeeper, saying, 'Take care of him, and whatever more you spend, I will repay you when I come back.' Which of these three, do you think, proved to be a neighbor to the man who fell among the robbers?" The answer is obvious: the good Samaritan. It was the person who was despised, not the supposedly godly people. Instead, it was the person who was looked down upon who ended up being generous, loving, and compassionate. Generosity is a powerful quality.

We may not have anything happen to us that is quite as dramatic as this, but I like to think that if Christians see a similar situation, we would be willing to do the same. There are all kinds of excuses we could make for not doing anything, just as the priest and the Levite did. Perhaps they were afraid the robbers were still there and would attack them or that the wounded man was faking his injuries to rob them. Maybe they thought the man deserved his wounds, that he had in some way brought it on himself. It would be easy to come up with reasons to cancel the godly quality of generosity. We all do. I have always wondered, when we look at people and say they don't deserve something, does God look at us and say we don't deserve what He has given us either? When we are impatient and judgmental, when we know nothing of others' lives, does God think about us and how we do not deserve all our blessings? I know there are people who take advantage of others, but I would rather be taken advantage of than be a selfish individual who refuses to help anyone because I might help someone who does not deserve it.

Mark 12:41–44 says of Jesus, "And he sat down opposite the treasury and watched the people putting money into the offering box. Many rich people put in large sums. And a poor widow came and put in two small copper coins, which make a penny. And he called his disciples to him and said to them, 'Truly, I say to you, this poor widow has put in more than all those who are contributing to the offering box. For they all contributed out of their abundance, but she out of her poverty has put in everything she had, all she had to live on.'" The widow literally gave her last penny. That is generosity. All the others had made a great show of putting money into the offering box. They wanted to be seen giving large amounts and to be admired. "Beware of practicing your righteousness before other people in order to be seen by them, for then you will have no reward from your Father who is in heaven. Thus, when you give to the needy, sound no trumpet before you, as the hypocrites do in the synagogues and in the streets, that they may be praised by others. Truly, I say to you, they have received their reward. But when you give to the needy, do not let your left hand know what your right hand is doing, so that your giving may be in secret. And your Father who sees in secret will reward you" (Matthew 6:1–4). We do not want to be giving just so that others will notice us. We should give generously, but as quietly as possible.

In Acts 16:13–15, we read of Paul and Silas as they visited the city of Philippi. "And on the Sabbath day we went outside the gate to the riverside, where we supposed there was a place of prayer, and we sat down and spoke to the women who had come together. One who heard us was a woman named Lydia, from the city of Thyatira, a seller of purple goods, who was a worshiper of God. The Lord opened her heart to pay attention to what was said by Paul. And after she was baptized, and her household as well, she urged us, saying,

'If you have judged me to be faithful to the Lord, come to my house and stay.' And she prevailed upon us." Opportunities to be generous come our way all the time.

Have you ever been in the position when you purposed in your heart to give to God, and then Sunday comes, and it has been a hard week, and you Think, *Should I cut back on my giving today?* Or perhaps you go ahead in faith and give what you had decided upon anyway. I encountered that situation more than once when I was young, and every time I went ahead and gave what I had planned on, regardless of how the week went, God blessed it. God loves generous givers. We cannot out-give God. He has already given us His best, so certainly He will give us what we need when we need it. That may not sound like good financial sense, but sometimes what we do — believing in God and His power, having faith against all odds — doesn't always make good sense. But when we do, God blesses us.

The churches in Macedonia were taking up a collection for the poor saints in Jerusalem. Paul, in writing to the church at Corinth regarding this collection, said "they gave themselves first to the Lord and then by the will of God to us" (2 Corinthians 8:5). Once we give ourselves and our possessions to God, recognizing that we own nothing and that it all is God's, then generosity becomes as natural as breathing. What we have is a gift from God. He has given us our health, our talents, and our opportunities, so without Him, we would not be where we are.

The most generous person I have ever known was my mother-in-law. She didn't have much money, yet I have never seen anyone who loved to give more than she did. It was her life. She bought toys for all the children at church on their birthdays. If people were in need, she would send them money. After she died, and we were getting her mail, we received at least 50 letters a month that were appeals for giving because she gave to every organization that approached her. She might not have given much, but she was as generous as she was able to be. Her generosity was a blessing to all who knew her. I think if we are getting pleasure out of giving to someone else, bringing them happiness and giving them something they really need, that has to bring us contentment. We know we are doing what God wants us to do.

How are we to give? We should give liberally and generously, not grudgingly. The following Scriptures describe how we are to give:

> "Now concerning the collection for the saints: as I directed the churches of Galatia, so you are also to do. On the first day of every week, each of you is to put something aside and store it up, as he may prosper, so that there will be no collecting when I come" (1 Corinthians 16:1–2).

Prepare in advance for the opportunities that are going to come your way. Set aside some money that has a singular purpose: contributions to the church and charity for any opportunities you encounter during the week.

"For you know the grace of our Lord Jesus Christ, that though he was rich, yet for your sake he became poor, so that you by his poverty might become rich. And in this matter I give my judgment: this benefits you, who a year ago started not only to do this work but also to desire to do it. So now finish doing it as well, so that your readiness in desiring it may be matched by your completing it out of what you have. For if the readiness is there, it is acceptable according to what a person has, not according to what he does not have. For I do not mean that others should be eased and you burdened, but that as a matter of fairness your abundance at the present time should supply their need, so that their abundance may supply your need, that there may be fairness. As it is written, 'Whoever gathered much had nothing left over, and whoever gathered little had no lack'" (2 Corinthians 8:9–15). Jesus had everything, and He had a choice of whether to come to earth and sacrifice Himself for us. His decision was to follow the will of the Father, because He knew that was what was best. In response we are to give what we know we can.

"The point is this: whoever sows sparingly will also reap sparingly, and whoever sows bountifully will also reap bountifully. Each one must give as he has decided in his heart, not reluctantly or under compulsion, for God loves a cheerful giver" (2 Corinthians 9:6, 7). I don't know how it works; it's beyond my comprehension, but God says if we give sacrificially, out of love and for the right reasons and purposes, then He will give back to us for two reasons. He will bless us for our giving, and He will give us more, so we are able to give more.

The Bible says that God opens the portals of heaven and gives back to us. "Give, and will be given to you. Good measure, pressed down, shaken together, running over, will be put into your lap. For with the measure you use it will be measured back to you" (Luke 6:38). He gives back to us in proportion to how generously we give. Do you see how generosity trumps greed? Greed says "I want all I can get. I want everything I can possess, just for the sake of having it." Generosity says, "Thank You, God, for everything You have given me and everything You have done for me. I want to give back to You and give to others as You have, showing my love and appreciation for You."

The Lord asks us to give. It is not a choice. "Thus, *when* you give to the needy . . ." (Matthew 6:2, emphasis added). Jesus wants us to give for the right reasons, not to be seen by others. He wants us to practice benevolence. We give to the church, and the church benevolently gives to those in need. Sometimes we have the opportunity to directly give to those in need. We are obligated to give to the poor, and that makes us more like God.

"Whoever sows sparingly will also reap sparingly, and whoever sows bountifully will also reap bountifully" (2 Corinthians 9:6). We must give of our free will, not under compulsion. We must give because we know it is right, and it is what God wants. The Lord says that in the end, "Your Father who sees in secret will reward you" (Matthew 6:4). God sees everything and will reward us accordingly.

When do we give? "On the first day of every week, each of you is to put something aside and store it up, as he may prosper, so that there will be no collecting when I come" (1 Corinthians 16:2). We give when we come together as the church so that the church can continue its good works. The Bible teaches that Christian giving must be done cheerfully to be acceptable. There has been much research lately regarding giving and generosity and how it affects the brain. The conclusions are amazing. Professors Philippe Tobler and Ernst Fehr, both part of the Department of Economics at the University of Zurich in Switzerland, have done an exhaustive study over the course of four years. In an article titled, "Manipulating the dopaminergic membrane," they have found that generous, charitable, giving people have more peace and contentment. Certain centers in their brains are positively affected when they practice generosity. That is not why we give, but I am glad to know that is a by-product of it.

QUESTIONS

1. How is generosity the opposite of greed?

2. What are some ways God has been generous to us?

3. How did Joseph treat his brothers and father in their time of need?

4. Discuss some of the lessons from Luke 10:30–36 concerning the good Samaritan.

5. How is generosity not tied to how much we have or the amount we give? (Consider the example of the poor widow in Luke 21:1–4.)

6. What are some opportunities that may have come to you to be generous to others?

7. Why do you think God loves a generous, cheerful giver?

8. What did the church in Macedonia give first?

9. Discuss 2 Corinthians 9:6, 7.

CHAPTER TEN

The Sin of Envy

ENVY IS TRULY A DEADLY SIN. HAVE YOU EVER HEARD THE expression "green with envy" or heard it described as the "green-eyed monster"? Jealousy and envy are closely related. In fact, the words *jealousy* and *envy* are often used interchangeably, and there is only a slight difference between them. In the late 1800s, Mark Twain referred to envious people as "green with envy" in a number of stand-up routines as well as in some of his writings. The phrase "green-eyed monster" comes from the Shakespeare play *Othello*. In the third act Iago says to Othello, "O beware, my lord, of jealousy; It is the green-eyed monster which doth mock the meat it feeds on." The green eyes were attributed to cats, because cats were considered the most envious of all animals.

The association of green with envy or jealousy goes back much further than these examples. The ancient Greeks thought that the color of a person's skin determined their health, and they placed envy in the same category as a sickness. They thought people who were envious were green, because when you were envious, the body would produce more bile, which caused a greenish tint to the skin. Whatever color envy is, it is a sin and creates many problems.

Socrates said, "Envy is the daughter of pride, the author of murder and revenge, the beginner of secret sedition and the perpetual tormentor of virtue. Envy is the filthy slime of the soul; a venom, a poison, or quicksilver which consumeth the flesh and drieth up the marrow of the bones." He had a low opinion of envy.

When we go to the Bible, we find that envy is listed with the worst of all considered sins. Galatians 5:19–21 says, "Now the works of the flesh are evident: sexual immorality, impurity, sensuality, idolatry, sorcery, enmity, strife, jealousy, fits of anger, rivalries, dissensions, divisions, *envy*, drunkenness, orgies, and things like these. I warn you, as I warned you before, that those who do such things will not inherit the kingdom of God." Envy is stacked right in the middle of all of the sins. It is a disastrous quality, harms everyone it touches, and causes people to say and do detrimental things.

Envy is one of those sins that is rarely every admitted. In fact, I think we rarely ever recognize it in ourselves. It often takes someone else pointing out to us that we may have envy in our lives. We don't want to admit it. Many people think envy is really not that bad, even though we know it is incredibly destructive. Paul lists envy as one of the major works of the flesh. Envy causes a lot of heartache, sorrow, and pain.

Envy is a spiritual sin and sickness. As with any sickness, there are symptoms.. Different sins have different symptoms. When you find someone who is putting someone else down constantly, it may be because they are envious or jealous of that individual. They may be envious of people who are better looking than they are, or who have more athletic ability. They might envy those who have a better job or position, better possessions, or more intelligence.

Envy is defined as "regret, jealousy, being sorry for another person's good fortune or achievement." When we envy someone, we not only want what the other person has, but we also don't want them or anyone else to have it at all. That may be the major difference between envy and jealousy. It isn't so much that we desire or want something, but it's that we don't want the person who does have it to have it. We wish them ill, or we try to put them down in some way or another.

This raises the question: "Is there anyone I envy?" It is hard to take an honest look at ourselves and ask this question. If there is someone we envy, we need to get rid of those feelings. As we study further, we will learn how to do this. We first need to identify the problem and then begin to work on it.

Pride was the first sin to enter into God's creation. Pride caused Adam and Eve to sin. Pride caused Satan to be cast out of heaven, because Satan wanted to be God. He wanted to take God's place. In Isaiah 14:12–14, Satan uses the words *I will* five times, describing how he wanted to take power away from God. Envy is the second sin mentioned in the Bible. It is the sin of Cain, of Joseph's brothers, of Saul and David. Saul became so envious and jealous of David that he wanted to kill him at all costs.

The Jews were so jealous of Jesus, of the crowds He attracted, the miracles He worked, and the people He healed, that the scribes and Pharisees wanted to kill Him. When Jesus appeared before Pilate and the priests began to make their case against Him, Scripture says that Pilate knew they were there out of envy (Matthew 27:18). We need to be careful that envy doesn't take hold in our lives.

Moses and Aaron were envied by the Israelites because of the power that had been given to them by God (Psalm 106:16). Envy is everywhere. It is people stabbing others in the back at work to get a position for which they may not be qualified, but they don't want anyone else to have. It is wanting something that someone else has so badly that we are willing to sabotage their getting it.

Why Envy?

Envy is close to jealousy and covetousness. But why are people envious? Why do humans envy the good fortune and blessings of others? First, it has to do with our not being content with how God made us. We are not content with where we are or who we are, and we become envious. We feel we have been cheated in some way, so we look at others and compare ourselves to them. One of the best and quickest ways to overcome envy is to stop comparing ourselves to other people. Instead, we should focus on ourselves and the talents and abilities God has given us. Remember the parable of the talents? Some had five, some just had one, but no one was judged on how many talents they had. Rather, they were judged on how well they used those talents. The man with the one talent would receive a reward equal to the reward of the five-talent man if he used that one talent to the glory of God and the benefit of humanity.It is important for us to understand that we should not compare ourselves to others.

> God has given each one of us what we have.
> He has made us who we are.

There is a second danger in comparing ourselves to others. We do not know just how happy or content another person is. We may envy what they have, but they may actually be miserable. They may not be what we assume they are, they may not have what we assume they have, and as a result, we envy something that would ultimately be bad for us. God has given each one of us what we have. He has made us who we are. I am disturbed by the concept of someone wanting to change their identity, trying to get rid of something that they feel is not right about themselves instead of accepting themselves as God made them. For example, there are men wanting to become women and women wanting to become men. An extreme case I heard of was a man thinking he should never have been born with a left arm, so he had surgery to have it removed. That is how sick we become when we begin to think we know more than God about the kind of people we should be.

We are wrong when we think we can out do God and His creation. It is in the acceptance of who we are, the talents we possess, what we can do (and not what we can't), what we can get and have legitimately (not what we desire to have illegitimately) that we will find the happiness, peace, and purpose that God intends for us. This is the only way it will ever happen. Do not look to others for your happiness. Do not compare yourself to others or judge yourself by someone else, especially their successes.

Envy causes a symptom that keeps us from loving as God wants us to love. First Corinthians 13:4 says, "Love does not envy." Conversely, if we envy, we cannot love as God wants us to love. We need to get rid of the envy, so we can have that perfect love that God wants us to have. You cannot love someone on whom you have wished evil. When you envy Someone, you wish evil upon them. We must be content with the circumstances of our lives. I think that should be a relatively easy and simple thing to do. The most miserable people I know are those who want what their abilities, talents, or resources won't allow them to have. They envy others, and that makes them unhappy. Envy is sorrow for another person's good fortune. If you see somebody who won't compliment anyone, it may be because they are feeling envy for the good fortune of others.

Family Envy

There is even envy in families. Siblings envy one another. This creates all kinds of problems in a home. We need to learn acceptance of who we are and what we have, doing the best we can with that. If we do this, we will find contentment and happiness.

Envy causes our ego, our wounded self-image, to want the worst for others and the best (that we do not deserve) for ourselves. The author C.S. Lewis started out as an atheist but eventually became one of the most prolific writers for Christian thought in the world. In his book *Mere Christianity*, he wrote, "Pride gets no pleasure out of having something, only out of having more of it than the next man. We say that people are proud of being rich, or clever, or good-looking, but they are not. They are proud of being richer, or cleverer, or better-looking than others." That can be said of both pride and envy. We have unrealistic expectations, and we feel like we deserve what we don't deserve and that we should have what we really do not need.

The Cure for Envy

Now the cure. I have already mentioned that we should stop comparing ourselves to others. We, as the church, are one body. We have many parts, but together we are one body. We should never be jealous of another part of the body. In 1 Corinthians 12:14–20. Paul says, "For just as the body is one and has many members, and all the members of the body, though many, are one body, so it is with Christ. For in one Spirit we were all baptized into one body — Jews or Greeks, slaves or free — and all were made to drink of one Spirit. For the body does not consist of one member but of many. If the foot should say, 'Because I am not a hand, I do not belong to the body,' that would not make it any less a part of the body. And if the ear should say, 'Because I am not an eye, I do not belong to the body,' that would not make it any less a part of the body. If the whole body were an eye, where would be the sense of hearing? If the whole body were an ear, where would be the sense of smell? But as it is, God arranged the members in the body, each one of them, as he chose. If all were a single member, where would the body be? As it is, there are many parts, yet one body."

We must understand that none of us can have all the talents. If we were all were the eye, we wouldn't be able to function. If all of us had what we in our minds considered to be the greatest abilities, talents, and resources, the rest of the body would fail. Not everyone can be a heart, or lung, or eye, or ear. But when you take all the talents that each of us possesses, given to us by God, we make up a whole, functional body to be used in His service.

I believe everybody has a talent. I don't believe there is anyone who cannot do something in God's kingdom and something to support themselves. We should be thankful for our individuality and the fact that we are able to use, in a special, particular way, whatever talent or resource we have. It doesn't have to be a great thing. You can lift up a person with just a phone call. You can bless someone and make them happy with just a note. Everyone has some sort of ability. We have several ladies in my home congregation who, though they suffer with health and other difficulties, find the time and have the ability to send encouraging notes. What a great gift and uplifting talent!

Another part of the cure for envy is to learn to be happy for the good that comes to others. Learn to love God first and your fellow man second. The best cure for any evil is to learn to love. We need to learn to be content, as we have already mentioned. Proverbs 19:23 teaches, "The fear of the Lord leads to life, and whoever has it rests satisfied; he will not be visited by harm." The Apostle Paul discovered the secret of contentment. He wrote, "I have learned in whatever situation I am to be content. I know how to be brought low, and I know how to abound. In any and every circumstance, I have learned the secret of facing plenty and hunger, abundance and need" (Philippians 4:11, 12).

Most of us want more than we need, and often we want more than what is good for us. Hebrews 13:5, 6 states, "Keep your life free from love of money, and be content with what you have, for he has said, 'I will never leave you nor forsake you.' So we can confidently say, 'The Lord is my helper; I will not fear; what can man do to me?'" This is a promise to all God's children, that He will take care of all our basic needs.

The cure for envy is to use the talents God has given us to the best of our abilities and to His glory and honor and to learn to be content with what God has given us.

QUESTIONS

1. Discuss the works of the flesh discussed in Galatians 5:19–21 and how envy finds its rightful place there.

2. What are some symptoms of an envious person?

3. Why do we envy others?

4. Who do you envy, if anyone?

5. Name some biblical examples of those who displayed envy or jealousy in their lives.

6. How are *envy*, *jealousy*, and *covetousness* similar?

7. Why is it true that if we truly love someone, we will not envy them?

8. How can envy create problems in one's family (example: Joseph and his brothers)?

9. What are some cures for envy?

10. How can the advice of Hebrews 13:5–6 help us avoid envy?

CHAPTER ELEVEN

The Virtue of Peace

HOW CAN A PERSON BE HAPPY IN A WORLD WHERE THERE IS so much discontentment? How can a person be happy when they are sick or suffering? How can you be at peace when you have pain so deep and hurtful that you cannot seem to get beyond it? How can you be happy in adverse circumstances, difficult situations, or around angry people?

When we are angry or discontented, we often commit other sins, often including assault or murder. Per *thesaurus*.com, there are 48 synonyms for anger and 20 antonyms for *anger*. The three antonyms I think are most applicable are peace, contentment, and pleasantness. These are the opposite of anger. Peace, to me, is at the top of the list. If we have peace in our minds and hearts, then everything else is better. It is, without question, a life-giving virtue.

Peace is a fruit of the Spirit (Galatians 5:22). It is a result of eliminating anger, frustration, and quarreling from our lives. Almost everyone wants peace. We want to feel that everything is okay, that there is nothing beyond the control of our own abilities and God's grace. We want to believe that most things are good in our lives even though there may be difficult and sometimes even bad elements. We need peace between nations and between individuals. We need to be at peace with God. Peace, especially personal peace, is absolutely essential for us to function normally. In a world of turmoil, hatred, bitterness, and unrest, it is often difficult to be at peace personally, yet it *is* possible. The Bible tells us that we are to seek peace and make it a part of our lives. There is nothing worse to me than the absence of peace of mind — worry, constant fearfulness, never being under control mentally. We worry about paying bills or buying food. Worry eats away at us. Where there is worry, there is an absence of peace. The more the worry, the less the peace.

There are those with illnesses or other physical problems who struggle every day with debilitating difficulties. These problems steal our peace, although I do believe for the Christian it is possible to find peace in the midst of serious and even deadly disease or difficulties. But it is a matter of knowing how, a matter of a relationship between us and our Maker, and a matter of believing that God knows what is best for us. I suppose that is the most difficult concept for us to accept. We pray, "Thy will be done," but when God's will may mean our own demise or the demise of a loved one, it is difficult to really believe it. But God will not visit us with anything that is beyond our ability to bear with His help (1 Corinthians 10:13).

Some find life so meaningless and difficult that they take their own lives. There are 45,000 suicides on average each year in the United States. That means each day about 123 people decide to take their own life. Life becomes so burdensome or painful that they simply feel they can't take it any longer. Add to that statistic the fact that 60 million Americans are on tranquilizers of one kind or another. Sixty million people find it difficult to make it through the day without medicating their reality. Some of these medicines are essential for those who have chronic mental or emotional problems, not caused by anything other than the body's chemical and hormonal imbalance. Others are painfully living with some physical ailment, but most of these people simply cannot cope with the daily pressures of life, so they turn to medication to take away that pain.

Did you know that 24 million people who are addicted to one kind of drug or another? Twenty-four million people get up every morning looking for their drug of choice, willing to do anything to get that drug to dull their senses and their pain (mental or emotional) to get through the day. Many would rather become a kind of zombie rather than address their issues and try to find an answer for them. In doing so, they become addicted to their drug of choice, spiraling their lives even further out of control and compounding their other issues.

The Bible teaches that Christians can and should have peace. "Peace I leave with you; my peace I give to you. Not as the world gives do I give to you. Let not your hearts be troubled, neither let them be afraid" (John 14:27). Peace is a part of the fruit of the Spirit that God gives us. As we understand that God will supply peace, and that we will never be tested or tempted beyond what we are able to bear (1 Corinthians 10:13), that doesn't mean that what we are able to bear isn't painful, difficult, or uncomfortable. Often, we turn to every other possibility first. We try to handle things ourselves and find that we are inadequate in every way to bring about a meaningful peace. We try drugs or alcohol, or we seek pleasure just to bring meaning or purpose to our lives. Some become extremely immoral, and as a result, compound their problems.

> God has a formula for peace, and it is free and accessible, but it can't be bought.

When you violate the will and Word of God, you will find that it only brings more problems. Yet we run in all directions looking for peace, purpose, happiness, and joy, and the majority of people never find it because they never go to the source, to the Creator, to the One who knows and understands us, and who has the answers. Millions of people would give everything they own for peace of mind. If they could simply find peace in their lives, they would be willing to become impoverished because peace would be better than wealth. But we cannot buy peace. God has a formula for peace, and it is free and accessible, but it can't be bought. We chase money and material things, thinking that they will bring us what we are looking for or give us what we need. We need material things to live, but they will never bring us what we need most — the purpose that God intends.

There are people who get drunk, stoned, or high day and night, thinking it will bring them peace. It never does. For the majority of my life as a therapist, I dealt with people who had addictions and mental and emotional problems, and they were looking for peace where it can never be found. Some think that the more they know, the more education they have, the easier time they will have finding peace. They become students, filling their heads with knowledge, but their hearts remain empty. Simply knowing facts or theories does not fill the God-void in our hearts. Just getting an education will never be enough to bring us peace, purpose, happiness, and joy. Peace cannot be bought with money, it cannot be acquired through chemicals or alcohol, and it cannot come about through knowledge. Peace is contingent on a close and right relationship with God.

The Bible says that when we become Christians, God will grant us a peace that passes human understanding. That passage used to be translated "that passes understanding," and I think that is true. It passes all understanding. This is something that people outside of Christ can never understand. They will never be able to comprehend it, because we are here not just for the ride on this earth, but as Christians, we are looking to eternity. We know that this is our pilgrimage, to prepare for a better way of life with our Father. We get ready here for there. Out in the world there are those who mock and degrade the cross, but it is in that cross, that sacrifice, that shedding of the blood that we find peace and salvation. The world will never understand it, but we do!

Christians sometimes find themselves in situations in which they are not at peace, which means we have to go inside our hearts and take a spiritual inventory to see what is wrong. If we are functioning as we should, we should at least have a minimum peace of mind. If it is not there, then we have something blocking it that we either haven't given up or we don't understand that is creating the problem. Even Christians can't live in sin and find peace. There has to be a resolution of the conflict between what God wants and what we are doing. When that conflict is resolved, then we find peace in our hearts and in our lives.

Have any of you ever known a time in the history of this country when there was less peace between nations and individuals? It is amazing to me. When I was growing up, patriotism was something everyone celebrated. Everyone was happy to be an American. Even though there were racial tensions and problems, those were being addressed. Today, if you don't think just like someone else, you are the enemy of that individual. Where there is an enemy, there is a war, and where there is a war, there is no peace. There are people who want war, because they want what they desire and don't care about anyone else. When I was growing up, I accepted many things without necessarily agreeing with them. I knew they were wrong, but I wasn't out bashing or berating people because of it. I accepted them as they were because not even God makes anyone do anything they don't want to do. We all have free will. We accept that there are sinners in the world, people who do not believe in God, people who will never believe that life is valuable, and people who do not agree with us on many issues. This does not mean that I will not get into a reasonable discussion with anyone and try to change their hearts and minds, but it does mean that we have a responsibility to live at peace with all men so much as is in us. "If possible, so far as it depends on you, live peaceably with all" (Romans 12:18). "Strive for peace with everyone, and for the holiness without which no one will see the Lord" (Hebrews 12:14). Yet there are people who do not want peace, and that makes it difficult to live in peace. We turn on the television and see people rioting and fighting, burning and looting. We must encapsulate ourselves in God to find peace in our own lives.

Peace Among Nations
In the past 4,000 years of recorded history, how many years of world peace do you think there have been? There have only been 288 years out of 4,000 when there has not been some conflict or war somewhere in the world. That is only eight percent of all recorded history during which time there has been peace among nations. We are a warring, fighting people. It seems to be innate, and certainly Satan is continually stirring us up, trying to get us to participate in conflict. Ninety-two percent of the time, there has been war somewhere in the world. In my own lifetime I have witnessed wars, although they were not always called that by our government, where soldiers were sent overseas to fight and die. We can go back further to World War I, the Civil War, the Spanish American War, the War of 1812, the Revolutionary War, the French and Indian War, and even more. It seems like our nation has always been involved in some sort of conflict somewhere. The Bible says, "'Peace, peace,' they say, when there is no peace" (Jeremiah 6:14). The reason there is no peace is because most of the world does not know about or care about God. Most of the world is involved in hatred, bitterness, tension, war, and all of the things that bring about hurt and harm.

We can go even further back than that to how early settlers disgracefully, in my judgment, took this nation away from the native Americans. We have always had a conquest concept of obtaining more and more. The Spanish and French had it, all under the name of Christianity and bringing Christ to the nations they went into and conquered, but what they really did was go to the world, taking Christianity to the people but also taking over their land. War, it seems, is a part of humanity. I am not saying that there are not justifiable wars. Throughout the Old Testament, God's people fought wars trying to bring about a more godly understanding of who we are and what we are.

With all our supposed advancements, it just goes to the core of my being to hear others say today, "We are more advanced and enlightened beyond any generation ever before. We know more, we are more intuitive, we are more scientific, we have built greater buildings and cities, we have cured all kinds of diseases, we have gone into space." But I tell you, we are no better from a peace of mind standpoint than Adam and Eve were. Today, we still commit the same sins and are guilty of the same transgressions. We still try to get around God's laws and ways in our lives. We still try to do everything ourselves. Hatred, malice, and war still exist today. Have we made any advancements in becoming better, more loving, kinder, more charitable people? Some have, and the majority of them are Christians. Look at the hospitals. Almost every hospital was started by a Christian group, a group who believed in God and wanted to help the sick as Jesus taught. Look at the orphanages and places that take care of the elderly. Most of them were started by Christians trying to do what Jesus asked us to do.

I remember when we began building Christian towers for the elderly throughout the brotherhood. This was an effort on the part of the church to take care of the elderly. I remember living next door to an orphanage in Morrilton, Arkansas that once was Harding

College, which moved to Searcy, Arkansas. It all started out as an effort to take care of orphans, which is what Jesus said we are to do. The world is not so much interested in these efforts. Almost all good works have come about because of God's people. I am thankful for that. God changes hearts and minds, taking away the pollution that is there, so we can see what our real purpose is — to love God with all our heart, soul, mind, and body, and to love each other as we love ourselves. We should take care of one another and be there for one another.

The natural man, without God, will never find true peace. The Christian who still harbors something that is opposed by God will find it difficult to achieve peace. People live in turmoil, restless, searching, trying any new fad or gimmick that comes along that they hope will bring them some sort of peace. But only God can provide the kind of peace that we really need. Only in Christ can we find forgiveness, which eliminates guiltand brings about peace. Only Jesus can give us purpose in life, telling us why we are here, what we are about, and where we are going when we leave this place. This gives us peace.

Peace With God

Peace comes with the right relationship between man and God. In fact, the Bible says He is our peace (Ephesians 2:14). Without Him, we will never find true peace. So many today are bewildered and confused, without peace. Isaiah 48:22 says, "'There is no peace,' says the Lord, 'for the wicked.'" If you are wicked, you will never find peace. If you ignore and abandon God, there is nowhere else you can find peace. Jesus says in John 14:27, "My peace I give to you. Not as the world gives do I give to you. Let not your hearts be troubled, neither let them be afraid." Do you want to know how to get over fear, how not to worry, how to find peace? Find Jesus, stand for what He stands for, do what He asks us to do, and you will find peace. But if you become a Christian and then spend every penny you have, borrowing from others without repaying them, then you will not find peace because you are not doing what God says. If you try to live an immoral life on Friday and Saturday night and then go to church on Sunday morning, you will never find peace. Being a part of Christ means doing what He wants us to do and only in doing so will we find peace.

We want to have peace of mind to be able to rest, not worry, and enjoy our lives. Let's give our lives to the Lord. The closer we come to Him, the more peace we will find. The further away we are from Him, even if we wear His name, the less peace we will have.

Philippians 4:6–9 says, "Do not be anxious about anything, but in everything by prayer and supplication with thanksgiving let your requests be made known to God. And the *peace of God*, which surpasses all understanding, will guard your hearts and your minds in Christ Jesus. Finally, brothers, whatever is true, whatever is honorable, whatever is just, whatever is pure, whatever is lovely, whatever is commendable, if there is any excellence, if there is anything worthy of praise, think about these things. What you have learned and received and heard and seen in me — practice these things, and the God of peace will be with you." These are the promises of God. Peace of mind is something that we all want. We all want lives without worry or anxiety. From time to time there will be events in our lives where something happens that shatters our reality for a while, but if we are grounded in the Lord, we will come back to our place of peace and contentment. We don't want to be burdened with the worries, problems, and difficulties that plague the world in general.

What do we have to do to get peace? First, we need to understand that God wants us to have true peace. God tells us not to worry and turn whatever is disrupting our peace over to Him. He is greater and more powerful than any problem we may have, and He wants to help.

Where do we begin to find peace? The most obvious answer is in God's Word. He does not want us worrying about anything. We are to take one day at a time, do everything we can to accomplish God's will that day, then turn whatever we cannot do over to Him. Philippians 4:6 says, "Do not be anxious about anything." I like the word *anything*. It means do not be anxious about anything at all. That encompasses all things. That means "don't worry." The word *anxiety* is often substituted for *worry*. In the Greek it means, "Don't be troubled" or "don't have unreasonable cares" about anything. In Matthew 6:25 we read, "Therefore I tell you, do not be anxious about your life, what you will eat or what you will drink, nor about your body, what you will put on. Is not life more than food, and the body more than clothing?" In Matthew 6, Jesus gives us the secret to overcoming worry and anxiety: "But seek first the kingdom of God and his righteousness, and all these things will be added to you. Therefore do not be anxious about tomorrow, for tomorrow will be anxious for itself. Sufficient for the day is its own trouble" (33–34). First Peter 5:7 tells us to "[cast] call your anxieties on him, because he cares for you." John 14:1 says, "Let not your hearts be troubled. Believe in God; believe also in me."

Useless worry, anxiety, fear, and doubt are all indicators that we may not trust God as we should and that we do not take Him at His word. In Philippians 4:6 we have an additional indication of how to achieve peace. "But in everything by prayer and supplication with thanksgiving let your requests be made known to God." Paul says "everything" here — that means nothing left out. Every care, problem, difficulty, sickness, sadness, or loss that you may have is of concern to God, from the smallest of our trials and tribulations up to the highest of our desires and needs. Romans 15:13 says, "May the God of hope fill you with all joy and *peace* in believing, so that by the power of the Holy Spirit you may abound in hope." The Spirit of God dwells in every Christian. He assists us as we live our daily lives. Acts 2:28:

"You have made known to me the paths of life; you will make me full of gladness with your presence." God is even preparing for our peace, happiness, and joy in the afterlife.

I am afraid that we trust in so many other things rather than God and His promises. We walk by sight and not by faith, and in doing so, we miss out on so many of the true blessings God wants for us. God wants to prove His love, concern, compassion, and care for us by helping provide for our needs, but we often pre-empt His intents, trying to do things entirely on our own, then end up turning to Him in desperation after we have tried everything else. Trusting God is a matter of faith. We don't have to worry about tomorrow, whether we will have enough money for our needs, whether we will be healed from an illness, whether we will get or keep a job. "In everything by prayer and supplication with thanksgiving let your requests be made known to God" (Philippians 4:6). Pray about the big and small things.

After we have prayed, Philippians 4:7, 8 says, "And the peace of God, which surpasses all understanding, will guard your hearts and your minds in Christ Jesus. Finally, brothers, whatever is true, whatever is honorable, whatever is just, whatever is pure, whatever is lovely, whatever is commendable, if there is any excellence, if there is anything worthy of praise, think about these things."

QUESTIONS

1. Discuss how personal peace, peace with God, and peace with one another is affected when we are envious.

2. How does our submission to God and His will allow us to be less envious?

3. What are some ways envy destroys our own personal peace of mind?

4. Where does peace come from (John 14:27)?

5. Can peace be bought or stolen?

6. What is meant by the statement, "God will grant us peace that passes understanding"?

7. Are the same feelings and sins responsible for the lack of peace between nations, peace between individuals, or personal peace?

8. Discuss Romans 12:18 and how we can effectively live this out in our lives.

9. How have most of the large humanitarian efforts to help the elderly, the needy, the widows and orphans begun?

CHAPTER TWELVE

The Sin of Anger/Wrath

ANGER IS A SIN THAT AFFECTS EVERY ONE OF US, AND IT'S something we must constantly check to make sure we're keeping it under control. A sin that leads to many other sins, anger can be a part of almost anyone's life, even any Christian's life. It destroys relationships with one another and with God.

Anger is uncontrolled temper. Wrath is the physical and mental abuse of anger. In Ezekiel 22:31 God says, "Therefore I have poured out my indignation upon them. I have consumed them with the fire of my wrath." That simply means that they were punished. God's anger was often stirred up by the Israelites and others who refused to do His will.

Not all anger is bad. In fact, there is a righteous anger, and it is sometimes difficult to tell the difference between good and bad anger. In Ephesians 4:26 we read, "Be angry and do not sin; do not let the sun go down on your anger." If you are angry, work it out, talk it out, and then put it aside. That is the way we are supposed to handle anger, but unfortunately that is not always the case. In 2 Thessalonians 1, we read about God's anger and what makes Him the angriest as well as what He will do about the people who abuse and persecute His people. Paul says God will rectify the problem of persecution of His people. He may do it right away, or He may wait until the judgment, but He will deal with it.

Those who abuse and persecute the people of God will experience not only His Anger, but also His wrath: ". . . since indeed God considers it just to repay with affliction those who afflict you, and to grant relief to you who are afflicted as well as to us, when the Lord Jesus is revealed from heaven with his mighty angels in flaming fire, inflicting vengeance on those who do not know God and on those who do not obey the gospel of our Lord Jesus. They will suffer the punishment of eternal destruction, away from the presence of the Lord and from the glory of his might" (2 Thessalonians 1:6–9). That is God's anger toward people who reject Him and who abuse His people.

Sometimes we may think we are not being treated fairly. In our world today, we are not always treated fairly as Christians. We can see an atmosphere of bitterness, resentment, and hatred toward people of faith. God assures us in 2 Thessalonians 1 that this will be avenged sooner or later.

In Mark 3:5 we find people who were ignorant, and as a result of that ignorance, they felt the sting of Jesus' anger. It was the Sabbath day, and Jesus came across a man with a withered hand. He healed the man, and people said, "How can you do this? It is the Sabbath!" Jesus replied that the Sabbath was made for man by God, so He, as a part of God, could control the Sabbath any way He wanted. It was an opportunity to express His deity and tell the people who He really was. Jesus' point was they had a preconceived idea of certain things they could and could not do. There were prohibitions set by God for the Sabbath day. But if their ox fell in a ditch on the Sabbath, would they get it out? Yes, any Jew would do so. They would take care of life and death issues on the Sabbath if needed. Jesus pointed out they had their own exceptions to the Sabbath rules. The people resented who Jesus claimed to be and wanted to destroy Him, taking every opportunity to hurt and discredit him. Their preconceived ideas led to prejudice and misunderstanding, and it angered our Lord.

There is justifiable anger. In Matthew, we find Jesus walking into the temple. As He enters, He sees all kinds of animals for sale, but not the best quality. People were taking advantage of others. There were also money changers, some of whom would cheat the people from other countries as they changed their money. The Bible says the anger of the Lord was aroused. "And Jesus entered the temple and drove out all who sold and bought in the temple, and he overturned the tables of the money-changers and the seats of those who sold pigeons. He said to them, 'It is written, "My house shall be called a house of prayer," but you make it a den of robbers'" (Matthew 21:12, 13). Sometimes in our practice of religion we may even do things that displease God. These people certainly did.

> We must be careful in choosing our angry battles to make sure they are not personal battles and instead they are godly, righteous battles.

There are times when we should be angry. Jesus had a right to be angry at what was happening in the temple. He had a right to cleanse the temple, because there was dishonesty there and people being swindled. This was at their place of worship, of all places. Jesus was angry. We should get angry about social injustice, governmental corruption, child abuse, persecution of Christians. Righteous anger is acceptable. Unless we get angry on occasion, we will never do anything about the wrongs of the world. We must be careful in choosing our angry battles to make sure they are not personal battles and instead they are godly, righteous battles.

We are made up of mind, body, and soul. Our body is the temple of God's Spirit. Our mind, our brain, our comprehension, all those are important. What hurts one part of us hurts every part of us. What is wrong for one part of us is wrong for every part of us. Some things are wrong for our minds, our bodies, and our souls; anger is one of those things.

Under the influence of anger, the brain improperly interprets sympathy, empathy, and other vital aspects of positive brain activity. When we are constantly angry and that anger is boiling over, it will make us unable to be sympathetic or empathetic. This means we are unable to put ourselves in another's place and feel what they feel. Anger interferes with many other positive virtues we should have.

Anger affects the body as well. There are many health risks associated with chronic anger, including hypertension, type 2 diabetes, coronary artery disease, muscle tension, back pain, TMJ, and immune system suppression.

When we are living in a state of anger, always mad and upset, it affects every part of us. You may remember V.P. Black, a preacher from Texas. He used limericks throughout his preaching to make his point. One of those I have remembered for many years is:

> The acid of anger does more
> to the container in which it is stored
> than to anyone on which it is poured.

The acid of anger will eat away at your mind, your body, and your soul. Prolonged, chronic anger can literally kill you. You may have known people who were constantly upset, angry, and combative, and you probably also found that those people had many health problems.

Spiritually, anger leads to many other sins. It leads to physical, mental, and verbal abuse. It destroys our relationships with God and each other. Chronic, unjustifiable anger is a deadly sin for anyone.

Some people say, "I just have a short fuse" or "I have a chip on my shoulder." The fact is, we can't blame unreasonable anger on anything other than our unwillingness to control it. We have the ability to control our anger. The Bible teaches that it is essential for the Christian to be in control of their anger.

There are many, many examples in the Bible of people whose anger led them to commit all kinds of sins. In Genesis 4:2–10 we read, "Now Abel was a keeper of sheep, and Cain a worker of the ground. In the course of time Cain brought to the Lord an offering of the fruit of the ground, and Abel also brought of the firstborn of his flock and of their fat portions. And the Lord had regard for Abel and his offering, but for Cain and his offering he had no regard. So Cain was very angry, and his face fell. The Lord said to Cain, 'Why are you angry, and why has your face fallen? If you do well, will you not be accepted? And if you do not well, sin is crouching at the door. Its desire is contrary to you, but you must rule over it.' Cain spoke to Abel his brother. And when they were in the field, Cain rose up against his brother Abel and killed him. Then the Lord said to Cain, 'Where is Abel your brother?' He said, 'I do not know; am I my brother's keeper?' And the Lord said, 'What have you done? The voice of your brother's blood is crying to me from the ground.'"

Here is an instance in which anger leads to physical violence and death. Anger is the primary cause of domestic violence. You've likely heard instances in which someone becomes so angry that they lose total control and kill or permanently injure someone else. When one is angry, the body releases the same hormones and toxins as it would in a fight-or-flight situation. It is also true that when a person is using alcohol or other drugs, the ability to control their anger is suppressed. Many times people are under the influence of drugs or alcohol when they do the worst they do in anger, because it suppresses those gauges that would keep them from doing wrong.

We read of Joseph and his jealous brothers in Genesis 37. Their jealousy developed into anger, which led them to want to kill him. They ended up selling Joseph into slavery. This is similar to the story of Cain and Abel, where the Scripture twice tells us that Cain became so angry that his "face fell." You could see his anger just by looking at him. This specifically in the Hebrew refers to the flaring of the nostrils, the redness of the face, and the drooping of the face, all of which are characteristics of extreme anger. When people become angry like that, they do things impulsively that they often regret later. We must learn to control our anger because if it's left unchecked. it will eventually kill us or cause us to harm someone else.

Saul was jealous of David. The women in the cities celebrated David by singing, "Saul has struck down his thousands, and David his ten thousands" (1 Samuel 18:7). When Saul heard this, he became angry and attempted to kill David. Moses was angry at the nation of Israel. He led the people around, they complained all the time, and they were in a drought with no water. God promised to provide water, bringing Moses to a rock and telling him to speak to the rock. Water would then flow out of the rock, enough for everyone. By this point, Moses was angry. Anger often causes us to go beyond what is reasonable, what we know we should do, and even what we are told to do. "Then Moses raised his arm and struck the rock twice with his staff. Water gushed out, and the community and their livestock drank. But the LORD said to Moses and Aaron, 'Because you did not trust in me enough to honor me as holy in the sight of the Israelites, you will not bring this community into the land I give them'" (Numbers 20:11, 12). Moses' anger caused him to lose the opportunity to lead the Israelites into the Promised Land.

The stoning of Stephen in Acts 7 is an example of mob anger, where someone incites and stirs up a group of people to anger. "When the members of the Sanhedrin heard this, they were furious and gnashed their teeth at him. But Stephen, full of the Holy Spirit, looked up to heaven and saw the glory of God, and Jesus standing at the right hand of God. 'Look,' he said, 'I see heaven open and the Son of Man standing at the right hand of God.' At this, they covered their ears and, yelling at the top of their voices, they all rushed at him, dragged him out of the city and began to stone him. Meanwhile, the witnesses laid their coats at the feet of a young man named Saul. While they were stoning him, Stephen prayed, 'Lord Jesus, receive my spirit.' Then he fell on his knees and cried out, 'Lord, do not hold this sin against them.' When he had said this, he fell asleep" (Acts 7:54–60). Once you get a mob stirred up, there is little that won't do. We have seen it recently in demonstrations in the street and riots on college campuses. Businesses are burned, cars are overturned, people are injured and sometimes killed — all because of out-of-control rage.

When Jesus was killed, the Pharisees and priests decided they had to get rid of Him. They had a preconceived idea that the Messiah would set up an earthly kingdom, and Jesus was not what they thought the Messiah would be. As a result, they literally hated the Son of God. They were the religious leaders and they should have recognized Him. They should have been able to look at the Old Testament prophecies and see that He fulfilled every one of them, but instead they wanted Him dead because they were angry.

We do the same thing. We get a thought or a notion — right or wrong, good or bad — and we carry it to the extreme. It causes us all kinds of problems. We see anger everywhere today. I have talked to a number of people assigned by the court to come to counseling over road rage. Talking in group sessions, and it's easy to identify those with a rage/anger problem. If anything didn't go their way, or didn't suit them, they would eventually be angry about. It is a real problem. Family abuse, child or spousal abuse, religious abuse, race rage — all kinds of anger and prejudices that lead to anger. There is instantaneous anger, which means that on the spur of the moment you become enraged. Sometimes we jump to conclusions when we do not have all the facts and become angry. As parents, we have probably all done this when we blame and even punish a child for something that he or she really didn't do, and we end up apologizing and asking for forgiveness when we finally have all the facts.

In Colossians 3 Paul writes, "Put to death, therefore, whatever belongs to your earthly nature: sexual immorality, impurity, lust, evil desires and greed, which is idolatry. Because of these, the wrath of God is coming. You used to walk in these ways, in the life you once lived. But now you must also rid yourselves of all such things as these: *anger*, *rage*, malice, slander, and filthy language from your lips. Do not lie to each other, since you have taken off your old self with its practices and have put on the new self which is being renewed in knowledge in the image of its Creator. Here there is no Gentile or Jew, circumcised or uncircumcised, barbarian, Scythian, slave or free, but Christ is all, and is in all.

> Therefore, as God's chosen people, holy and dearly loved, clothe yourselves with compassion, kindness, humility, gentleness and patience" (Colossians 3:5–10).

We have control over our lives, our bodies, and our situations. We can put off the old things and put on the new.

Why do we get angry? We need to analyze what is going on in our lives. There are many reasons we might be angry—some we have more control over than others. I have been working recently with a person who has dementia, and it seems like anger becomes a part of dementia, especially in the more advanced stages. Medication must be prescribed, and it does help, but anger still is a problem for these people. Secondly, I simply say to do what Ephesians, Colossians, and Galatians say — just stop it!

Bob Newhart was one of my favorite TV shows many years ago because he portrayed a therapist. In one episode, he was working with a woman who was making every excuse for why she was angry and upset all the time. Bob Newhart listened to her patiently, and when she asked him, "What do I do? How can I get this under control?" he replied, "Just stop it!" Today Dr. Phil is what is called a "reality therapist." He doesn't go all the way back asking you to dredge up everything that has ever happened to you in your entire life because bad things have happened to all of us. We do, however, have to learn what is controlling us and how we can gain control of what is best in our lives. The best way to do it is to just quit being angry — to stop it! Along with that, we must have help from God. We pray to God, confessing our problems and our sins, and we ask God to cleanse us and forgive us, and then we seek the help of the Holy Spirit in our lives to guide us.

QUESTIONS

1. What is the definition of *anger*?

2. Is anger always bad?

3. What are some reasons why we become angry?

4. When should we be righteously angry?

5. How does anger affect us physically and mentally?

6. How does anger affect us spiritually?

7. What are common excuses for anger?

8. How can anger lead to physical and mental violence?

9. What was the result of Joseph's brothers' jealousy, envy, and anger?

10. What are other biblical examples of adverse problems resulting from anger?

11. How do we get rid of anger in our lives?

CHAPTER THIRTEEN

The Virtue of Patience

"MAY THE LORD DIRECT YOUR HEARTS TO THE LOVE OF GOD and to the steadfastness of Christ" (2 Thessalonians 3:5). Love seems to be a prerequisite to patience. We are willing to extend our patience, good behavior, and forgiveness to what we love and care about most. Love is the foundation upon which patience and most other virtues are built. Patience is defined as "the capacity or ability or habit or fact of bearing pain or trials calmly, without complaint." It is rather easy to be patient when things are going our way, but amid our trials and difficult situations, our patience often suffers.

Our English word *patience* is often translated in the Bible as *longsuffering*, *endurance*, or *perseverance*. In a real way, patience is being slow to become angry. Paul tells us that patience is one of the fruits of the Spirit. God's indwelling Spirit helps us withstand many of the pressures, difficulties, and challenges of life. God is patient and longsuffering toward us.

Personal confession: I must admit that during my life, patience has been one of the more difficult fruits for me to acquire. I have prayed for patience; I have put forth human effort to get patience, but when I judge myself, I find I am still lacking in this required godly quality. Thankfully, God sends us situations to help us acquire the characteristics we need and pray to have. My God-sent help came in the form of a beagle puppy my wife insisted we get. We have always had dogs, sometimes as many as three at once, and our previous canine companions have always been easily trained and well-behaved. Our most recent addition, however, has proven to be the exact opposite of the other dogs. She is self-willed, extremely determined, and, at five months, she pretty well runs the house. It isn't easy at 78 years old to get up every morning at 5:00, rain or shine, hot or cold, whatever the weather conditions, and walk this cute but determined puppy until she decides to do her duty. I have noticed over the past few months that my patience, after having taken an initial dip, has recently begun to increase, and I am able to demand less of her and expect more of myself. Maybe it isn't too late to teach this old dog new tricks inspired by our new, young dog.

Patience, as one of the results of God's Spirit living in us, requires that we do everything possible to acquire this godly gift of disposition. The Apostle Paul wrote often of the need for patience or endurance. It may be because he was the recipient of God's patience and longsuffering toward him. While he was persecuting, abusing, imprisoning, and even consenting to killing Christians, God was patient, and His patience proved to be justified as Paul became one of the principal missionaries and evangelists to the early church. Paul, having received the patience of God, understood the need for us to be patient with one another. "May the God of endurance and encouragement grant you to live in such harmony with one another, in accord with Christ Jesus" (Romans 15:5).

In all our relationships, patience becomes one of the greatest virtues. When we are young and dating, when we are older and married, when we are dealing with our children or interacting with friends, even when we are in conflict with those with whom we disagree, we always need patience. There are many problems associated with our being impatient. Certainly the spiritual problems are obvious; think about times you've flown off the handle and said or done things that were far from Christ-like. Physically, there is stress on the heart that often leads to high blood pressure. Socially, many lose good friends over harsh words and hurt feelings.

James wrote, "Count it all joy, my brothers, when you meet trials of various kinds, for you know that the testing of your faith produces steadfastness. And let steadfastness have its full effect, that you may be perfect and complete, lacking in nothing. If any of you lacks wisdom, let him ask God, who gives generously to all without reproach, and it will be given him. But let him ask in faith, with no doubting, for the one who doubts is like a wave of the sea that is driven and tossed by the wind. For that person must not suppose that he will receive anything from the Lord; he is a double-minded man, unstable in all his ways" (James 1:2–8).

Sometimes we are not prepared for the blessings of the Lord. We have to wait on God, in His own time and in His great wisdom to supply what we are lacking. Often we have to be transformed by difficulties, trials, and tribulations of various kinds. As my father once said to me before giving me a well-needed spanking for doing the same thing over and over again, "Larry, I'm sorry that you are such a slow learner."

Many of us are slow learners when it comes to developing the characteristics we should possess or getting something we think we need but haven't received, even after praying often about it. Waiting on God is not easy, but God in His infinite wisdom understands when we are ready to receive. "Be still before the Lord and wait patiently for him; fret not yourself over the one who prospers in his way, over the man who carried out evil devices! Refrain from anger, and forsake wrath! Fret not yourself; it tends only to evil" (Psalm 37:7, 8).

Patience is an essential quality for every Christian. It helps in every relationship and situation. It causes us to be more God-like, and it offers us hope. "For whatever was written in former days was written for our instruction, that through endurance and through the encouragement of the Scriptures we might have hope" (Romans 15:4).

Contentment, when translated from the Greek, means "individually sufficient or satisfied." Many of the Stoic philosophers defined *contentment* as "the ability to be free from material wants and needs." Some philosophers believe the ability to find contentment regardless of one's surrounding circumstances to be the epitome of all virtues. Contentment may also include the ability to be free from the temptations of excess and opulence and to be able to happily function with only the necessities of life. *Contentment* does not mean complacency or laziness. Each of us should do our best in everything. The Bible teaches that we should work hard and use our talents and abilities.

Contentment comes by realizing that God is all-sufficient and that we can trust Him to meet all of our needs. This was the main thrust of Jesus' teaching in the Sermon on the Mount concerning not being anxious, but always recognizing that if we are doing what we should be and living the life to which He has called us, He will see that our basic needs are met.

Paul had learned how to have great abundance and also how to be content in great need. "I know how to be brought low, and I know how to abound. In any and every circumstance, I have learned the secret of facing plenty and hunger, abundance and need" (Philippians 4:12). The key to this phenomenon was revealed in verse 13: "I can do all things through him who strengthens me." Once we believe that our Lord is sufficient to every need and that He loves us and will be with us in every circumstance of life, then we can relax and be content with where we are at that moment.

We need to learn how to get along when we have great abundance as well as when we are in need. Sometimes our abundance leads us away from God rather than toward Him. We become self-sufficient, arrogant, complacent, and the temptation to drift from God can come in both the good times and the bad. We should always be thankful for where we are in life. Sometimes it is the lean circumstances of life that lead us to introspection and cause us to correct whatever attitudes or conduct may be amiss in our lives. We need to be thankful for the good that God grants us, the blessings we receive, and also for the chastisement and correction that He offers when we miss the mark. We need to be thankful every day of our lives for all He has given us and done for us. We should be thankful for every meal we eat and offer our thanks, no matter where we are or in whose company we are. We should be thankful for our clothing, for our shelter, for our heat and air conditioning, and every other blessing that we so often take for granted. We can learn from God's interaction with the Israelites — protecting them, guiding them with the cloud by day and pillar of fire by night, feeding them with the quail and manna, defining *sin* and *righteousness* for them through the Ten Commandments, and patiently loving and caring for them even in their ingratitude, pride, arrogance, rejection, and condemnation. God always showed His mercy to them, but the Israelites seldom showed their appreciation for or contentment with the blessings of God. They always wanted more and better, and sometimes they just wanted different.

What anxieties would be relieved, what worry would be overcome, what doubt would find resolution if only we could learn the lesson of contentment! There are people who have so much more than they could ever need and whose money and worldly possessions will greatly outlive them. In their discontentment they accumulated great riches on earth, but laid up few treasures in heaven. And in their discontentment, they made bitter choices that will affect eternal destinies. More just for the sake of more is seldom, if ever, a good choice.

We have lost the blessing that comes from sacrifice. We don't want to give up anything, but we want to get everything. Sacrifice can be one of the great keys to contentment.

Contentment's Opposite

The opposite of *contentment* is *discontentment*, which results in a restless dissatisfaction with our lives and circumstances. Dissatisfaction is one of the major causes of divorce. It is one of the primary motives of addictions such as drugs, alcohol, over-shopping, or gambling. Some people cannot find even a moment of contentment. They are constantly changing everything around them and about themselves. This compulsive rearranging of one's life and circumstances causes us to be blinded to the real need, which is to fill the hole in our soul, heart, and mind with the Creator Who made us, understands us, and has provided the keys to contentment for us. Seeking to change our circumstances, thinking that will make us feel whole, complete, or acceptable is often a dead-end trail. Just changing the car you drive, the color of your kitchen, the carpet in your bedroom, your job, your spouse, your friends, your location, or your hobbies will somehow automatically bring you the peace and contentment you seek is unrealistic. The only changes that should be made purposefully in our lives are those that will make us better people, more righteous and God-like, more helpful and generous. It is in becoming selfless and not selfish that we find contentment. It is in doing more for others and less for ourselves that we find real purpose and peace. If you live for yourself and for your own satisfaction and pleasure, you will never know the true contentment God offers. If you live a life of righteousness and service to God, it doesn't matter if you are rich or poor, married or single, or any other worldly variable, you will find God's perfect contentment. We need to remember that "where your treasure is, there your heart will be also" (Matthew 6:21).

One of the secrets of contentment is to, in every circumstance, think about God's power, love, and ability to meet any and every need we as His children may ever have. Trust God, stop being anxious, stop worrying about things which will probably never happen and, if they do happen, will find their resolution in the mercy, grace, and comfort of God.

> "Not that I am speaking of being in need, for I have learned in whatever situation I am to be content. I know how to be brought low, and I know how to abound. In any and every circumstance, I have learned the secret of facing plenty and hunger, abundance and need. I can do all things through him who strengthens me" (Philippians 4:11–13).

QUESTIONS

1. What is a biblical definition of *patience*?
2. What are some reasons why it is difficult to be patient?
3. Discuss God's patience and longsuffering for us.
4. What are some reasons why we are not content?
5. What are some other words which could be translated as "patience"?
6. How are you patient with others?
7. How has God shown patience toward us?
8. How does trusting God produce contentment?

Bibliography

Bridges, Jerry. *The Blessing of Humility*. Navpress, 2016.

Campolo, Anthony. *Seven Deadly Sins*. Narrated by Anthony Campolo. Vistamedia, 1987. Audiobook.

Dunnam, Maxie and Kimberly Dunnam Reisman. *The Workbook on the Seven Deadly Sins*. Upper Room Books, 1997.

Getz, Gene A. *The Measure of a Man*. Regal Books, 2004.

Graham, Billy. *Freedom From the Seven Deadly Sins*. Zondervan, 1955.

_____. *Peace With God*. Thomas Nelson, 1991. Grubb, Norman P. *Who Am I?* Zerubbabel Press, 1974.

Hale, Lewis G. *Seven Deadly Sins and Others Just As Deadly*. Hale Publications, 2000.

Hauerwas, Stanley. *The Character of Virtue: Letters to a Godson*. Wm. B Eerdmans, 2018.

Hodge, Charles B. *Amazing Grace!* 20th Century Christian, 1984. Maston, T.B. *Right or Wrong*. Broadman Press, 1955.

Valentine, Lynn. *The Power of Prayer*. Premium Press America, 2002.

Warren, Rick. *The Purpose Driven Life*. Zondervan, 2002.

Wilson, Jared C. Seven Daily Sins. LifeWay Press, 2012.

www.ingramcontent.com/pod-product-compliance
Lightning Source LLC
LaVergne TN
LVHW051523070426
835507LV00023B/3268